3RD REVISED EDITION

W9-CEP-830

CHINA
SURVIVAL GUIDE

How to Avoid Travel Troubles and Mortifying Mishaps

Larry and Qin Herzberg

Stone Bridge Press • Berkeley, California

Published by
Stone Bridge Press
P.O. Box 8208
Berkeley, CA 94707
TEL 510-524-8732 • sbp@stonebridge.com • www.stonebridge.com

Book design by Linda Ronan.
Front cover illustration by Lloyd Dangle.

LIBRARY OF CONGRESS CATALOGING-IN-PUBLICATION DATA
Herzberg, Larry.
    China survival guide : how to avoid travel troubles and mortifying mishaps / Larry and Qin Herzberg. —3rd ed.
        p. cm.
    ISBN 978-1-61172-010-5 (pbk); 978-1-61172-552-0 (ebk).
    1. China—Guidebooks. I. Herzberg. Qin. II. Title.
    DS705.H47 2007
    915.104'6—dc22
                2007014401

Contents

Preface to the Third Edition

The first edition of this book was published in 2008. Although most of its information and advice still held true, based on our trips to China in the summers of 2009 and 2010 we presented a revised edition in 2011 with updated information on prices, the improved subway systems in Beijing and Shanghai, and Internet use. We also added a list of the best places to visit in China and a section on recommended books and movies.

We now offer a newly revised edition of our book, based on our travels around China during the summer of 2013. We have updated quite a bit of information and added an entire chapter on train travel as well as much more travel advice. The travel infrastructure in China has greatly improved in recent years, along with a dramatic increase in the overall standard of living. Some of the problems we mention in this book are becoming less visible in Beijing and Shanghai, Guangzhou, or Shenzhen. However, most of our advice should be useful today everywhere in China, especially outside of those very largest and most modernized cities. Our book is particularly essential for those who are not traveling on a guided tour where everything is arranged for them.

China remains a place of countless wondrous sights and adventures, with travel around the country made even easier and more pleasant than when we first published our guide. Our hope is that you will journey there soon and experience it for yourselves, and that when you do, our book will have helped you on your way.

Happy travels (or, as the Chinese say, "May you enjoy favorable winds")!

Acknowledgment

Our recent trips to China, upon which the updated information in this book is based, were made possible by generous grants from the David and Shirley Hubers Asian Studies Program of Calvin College, and by the National Endowment for the Humanities. We would like to gratefully acknowledge the significant financial support they have given us and to applaud the work they do.

Qin and Larry Herzberg
November 2013

Welcome to China!

Everyone we know is going to China these days. Or so it seems.

There are the business people who now travel frequently to China for their jobs, dealing with everything from office furniture and shoes to Amway products. There are the staff members at our college, who are heading to China to adopt a Chinese baby. The Women's Chorale from our school just returned from performing at Christian churches in Beijing and Xian. Four of our fellow professors, with several of our students to assist them, are about to head to China this summer to tutor English teachers from the Chinese countryside. Each summer we continue to arrange work opportunities for our students in China, which range from teaching English to working in a Chinese company. And then there are the countless friends of ours and parents and grandparents, uncles and aunts of our students, who all either just came back from a two-week trip to China or are just about to go. When we began to teach Chinese at our college in the early 1980s, almost no one was headed for China. Now going to China has become almost as common as a trip to England or France. China has captured everyone's fancy like never before. As kids, we were told that if we dug a hole in our backyards, sooner or later we'd end up in China. This always made us pause and wonder. Thanks to the miracle of airplane flight, you can now make it to China from anywhere in the United States within twenty-four hours. And you can arrive without sand in your britches.

Thinking of traveling to China? You're not alone. China now ranks as the third most visited country in the world (up from the two-hundredth or so most visited country in 1970, when China was still "closed" to most foreign visitors). Well over a hundred million people from all over the world traveled to China in 2006. Only two million of them were Americans, but that's two million more than went to the "Middle Kingdom" only one generation earlier. After decades of internal and external conflict, China was a geographical and political hot spot. It wasn't until 1972 that President Richard Nixon visited the country, met Mao Zedong, and captured the interest of the West. Economic reforms under Deng Xiaoping just a few years later finally helped open China to American tourists—and McDonald's.

Every culture has its own undisputed contributions to world history of which they can proudly boast. One of China's greatest contributions is its cuisine. If you've never had Chinese food in China, you've simply never really had Chinese food. What's that you say? You can drive over to Chinatown in Manhattan and eat Chinese food 'til the water buffalo come home? It's easy. Why settle for a pale imitation of Peking duck here at home when you can sample the real thing in China. Why eat ordinary pot stickers, as they are commonly called in American Chinese restaurants (where they are stuffed only with pork and cabbage), when

you can taste hundreds of varieties of *guotie* and *jiaozi* (savory pan fried and steamed dumplings), amid the colorful streets and alleys of Beijing or Shanghai? Of course, there are other reasons to visit China. There's history, for example. China is a very old place. Dynasties have come and gone. Uncounted millions of people have walked on its soil. While the United States, for instance, tracing its origins back to the earliest settlements in North America, can claim maybe four hundred or so years of history, China has over four thousand. For the history buff, China is the place to see. We Americans do have some important historical sites, but most tend to be small and intimate. China is all about big spaces, and the relationship of man-made objects to their natural surroundings. Nowhere is this more evident than at the Great Wall. Taking in the view at Badaling Pass, one of the more popular spots for tourists, you can see the wall running in the distance, until it goes behind the next hill. Then, you notice that the wall continues on to the next hill, and the next, and the next, as far as you can see.

Egypt is also an ancient civilization whose historical longevity is on par with China. Take their most famous monuments, the pyramids. These tombs of the Pharaohs are truly among the wonders of the ancient world. But if you get tired of seeing so

many tombs all pretty much made in the same shape, visit China for a look at an entirely different kind of tomb. The first emperor of China had a giant mausoleum built for himself beneath the ground with only a gigantic mound to mark the spot. He had around eight thousand life-size clay soldiers made to guard his tomb, each modeled after one of the soldiers in his army. These terra-cotta warriors have stood guard in rows buried in the clay of northwest China for 2,200 years. When they were unearthed in the mid-1970s, the discovery was called the archaeological find of the century.

You can visit Europe to see many palaces of kings and queens. England has Buckingham Palace, France the magnificent Palace at Versailles, and Germany boasts the Palace of Frederick the Great. None of these countries, however, has a palace that can compare in scope and grandeur to the Forbidden City in Beijing, home of emperors for more than five hundred years. According to lore it was supposed to have 9,999 rooms (it was said only heaven could have 10,000 rooms), with nine throne rooms. When compared to the terra-cotta warriors, for example, The Forbidden City, for all its size and scope, is still relatively "new" as far as Chinese landmarks go. Even though no one lives there today, you can sense the spirits of many generations of Chinese emperors long gone.

China is also worth visiting for the scenery. Like the U.S., which it resembles in size, China has some of the most beautiful and remarkable scenic spots in the world. The kinds of places where your jaw just drops and you try to find words while fumbling for your camera. Enjoy mountains? In China, mountains are sacred places. Huangshan and Taishan are two of the most popular. China borders the Himalayas, of course, but for something more down to earth, take a river cruise to see in real life what you've only seen in photographs: the stunning karst topography of Guilin and the Li River in southern China. There are the unusual mountain formations of Zhangjiajie in Hunan Province, and the aptly named Stone Forest in Kunming. Few national parks in the U.S. can equal the magnificence of China's Jiuzhaigou National Park, with crystal-clear pure mountain lakes and mountains reminiscent of Glacier National Park. Believe it or not, China also has its own version of the Grand Canyon: the Nujiang Canyon in Yunnan Province, an area that has often been called Shangri-La. It has also become one of the country's most popular tourist attractions.

Not everyone who visits China is there solely as a tourist. What's the fastest growing economy in the world today? It's China. No matter what your profession, you should be interested in what happens in China. Executives from Tokyo to New York, to London to New Delhi are converging on China; they want to be

in on the next "economic miracle."

There are other reasons people visit China. One of the most heartwarming of all is to adopt a Chinese baby, almost all of them are girls. Thousands of people from all over the world have come to China each year to bring a little Chinese child back to their country to be part of their family. Thriving communities of adoptive families and support groups have sprung up all over the world. Even with new, stricter rules for prospective adoptive parents now being put in place, China is still the country with the largest number of overseas adoptions. Every year that we've traveled back to China, we've stayed at a hotel in Beijing where there were many couples from Argentina or the Netherlands or the United States who had just adopted a Chinese toddler and were getting ready to go back home. It was hard to get through the line for the breakfast buffet due to all the strollers spread out all over the dining room. Americans alone adopted around four thousand Chinese youngsters in 2009. It's wonderful to see these loving, multiracial families that are common all around our west Michigan community.

The majority of visitors to China still travel with a tour group. Everything is arranged. No tickets to buy, no hotel reservations to make, no worrying about what plane or train or bus to take to your next destination, and no lines to stand in. Your tour guide will handle all that for you, and a driver in an air-conditioned bus will take you to all the interesting sites. That's fine for most people, but with more and more solo travelers, couples, or those traveling with family and friends, there is a strong desire to go off the beaten path, away from the air-conditioned buses, and away from the "arranged" tour. If you are one of those people who wants to see China on your own terms, you also have to be able to manage pretty much everything yourself.

You may be taking planes, trains, buses, and taxis. You will need to check yourself into your hotel, order a meal from a restaurant, or buy something in a store. In each case, you will encounter people. All of them (or nearly all) will be Chinese. Depending on where in the country you go, people will speak different dialects. The prevalent dialect is simply called "Guoyü," in places like Taiwan, or "Putonghua," in China (literally: "national language" and "common speech," respectively). This dialect is also commonly called "Mandarin" in English, and is the official language of China.

We've written this book to help inform others, as well as to help us partially relive the thrill of travel: meeting people from a different culture and getting to know them using whatever combination of language and gestures you have at your disposal. The only problem in China is that there are so many people to get to know. Sometimes it seems that at least a million of them are trying to shop in the same market you're shopping in or trying to buy tickets for the same train that you want to take. You came to

China wanting to "rub elbows" with the locals, but find that your elbows are a bit sore at the end of each day from all the people you've bumped into walking down the street. Maybe because every Chinese grows up with 1.3 billion other Chinese all around them, they have to learn to push and shove to get on that bus, or to crowd the train ticket window.

In short, not everything is rose-colored when it comes to traveling by yourself in China. There are unique challenges you must face, but should this discourage you from going? Absolutely not! You just need to be psychologically prepared for the little roadblocks of life that China will throw at you. Fortunately, there is nothing terribly serious for the typical tourist to worry about in China. Keep your wits about you, never lose your temper, and above all, keep a sense of humor.

In this book you'll find practical advice for how to make your way through China with good grace. The problems we talk about are for the most part neglected by most travel guidebooks. We tell you what hassles and headaches you might encounter and how to best deal with them. We also try to provide cross-cultural insight as to why those hassles and headaches exist in China in the first place. We hope to help identify potential problems before they affect you; and if you should find yourself in a potentially awkward situation, we hope that we can get you out of it with hopefully very little drama. We like to think our book will prepare you for unexpected cultural encounters by giving you an insider's look at China. Even if you never plan to visit the Middle Kingdom, perhaps you'll enjoy getting a new perspective on a country so different from your own. For those of you who venture to go, just keep in mind the dozens of invaluable tips we provide and you'll come back with nothing but happy memories and lots of great pictures. Let's visit China together in the pages that follow.

Larry and Qin Herzberg
Chinese Language Faculty, Calvin College
Grand Rapids, Michigan

A Note on Pronunciation

In using our Western alphabet to spell Chinese words, we have used two different methods. For each word or phrase we first give the standard transliteration that is now universally accepted. The officially recognized system of romanization is known as hanyu pinyin, or, simply, pinyin. If you've studied Chinese, chances are you'll be able to use pinyin. For those of you new to the Chinese language, we've also included our own unique transliteration of the words in parentheses. This should help you pronounce the words correctly.

Two common Chinese words that are usually pronounced incorrectly here in the U.S., by nearly all television and radio broadcasters, are the words "Beijing" and "yuan." The "j" in the name of China's capital city is not pronounced with the soft "j" sound like *Je suis* in French. The Chinese language lacks that sound entirely. The "j" in "Beijing" is pronounced like the "j" in "jingle."

The yuan is China's currency, just as the dollar is ours. It is not pronounced "you-anne" or "you-awn." It is pronounced "you-when," or "U.N." when said quickly as if it were one syllable.

A User's Guide to the Chinese Restroom

You've arrived at the airport in China. You feel refreshed and exhilarated after a short ride on the plane directly from your hometown. After all, you slept most of the way on a reclining leather seat the size of a twin bed, and sampled roast pheasant and fine French wine.

This statement might be true if your hometown happens to be Tokyo and you can afford a first-class seat. If so, this book might not be for you. More likely, you took a long-haul flight in an economy-class seat from San Francisco, Seattle, or Los Angeles. If you are like us, from the Midwest, then you had an additional flight: from your hometown airport to Chicago, Detroit, Denver, or some other major U.S. hub, then waited for a connection to your international flight. Depending on your carrier, you could be in for anywhere from ten to fifteen hours of total flight time to get to China. Flights originating overseas can land in Beijing, Shanghai, Guangzhou, Shenzhen, and Chengdu. Beijing Capital Airport or Shanghai Pudong Airport are the major points of entry for most international flights. You disembark from the plane and are ushered into the immigration area. As you shuffle down the corridor, until recently you might have encountered a uniformed officer aiming a gun-like instrument at your forehead. In any case, don't panic. What this officer is doing is taking everyone's temperature with a state-of-the-art infrared digital thermometer. Chances are if anyone is running a high fever, they may be taken aside for medical evaluation before being allowed to enter the country. Seldom do we emerge from a long-haul flight in the best of shape, but the vast majority of travelers have nothing to fear from this seemingly invasive procedure.

By all appearances, most of China's cosmopolitan airports are now state-of-the-art structures; they resemble nothing like the crumbling, utilitarian buildings of old, which were nothing more than immense waiting rooms practically right on the tarmac itself, where planes roll to a stop within a few feet of the building. Everything about China's new airports gives you the impression that the country has taken great strides at modernizing its infrastructure. And that is true in the Beijing and Shanghai Airports, but only since just before the Olympics in 2008. That's when the Chinese government remodeled the facilities in order to accommodate the hordes of foreign visitors used to having toilet paper provided in the stalls, with automatic flush, and with soap and hot water in the sinks. Do not let this mislead you into thinking that these are the kind of washrooms you'll find in the rest of China. A quick trip to the restroom in most places in China will put you squarely back in reality. You're not in Kansas anymore, but in China. Things are different here.

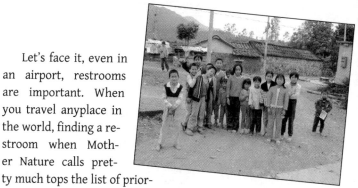

Let's face it, even in an airport, restrooms are important. When you travel anyplace in the world, finding a restroom when Mother Nature calls pretty much tops the list of priorities. It's hard to enjoy any part of your trip if you need to use one but there are none in sight. When it comes to China, talking about restrooms is very important, especially when seconds count. Memorize these characters: 男 (Nán) is male, 女 (Nǚ) is female. Often they may be more prominently displayed than the words "Men" or "Women" or even the familiar gender-specific silhouettes we are accustomed to seeing. Not to worry, however, if you can't read the Chinese characters for the two gender choices. The general rule of thumb in almost all of China is "men left, women right," meaning that the men's restroom will be on the left-hand side and women's on the right. Only in the areas populated primarily by minority peoples is the opposite true.

If you're female, and at least half the human race is of that persuasion, then you have a special treat in store at some Chinese airport restrooms outside of the largest cities like Beijing and Shanghai. You may walk into one of the lovely modern stalls provided for you. Lulled into a sense of security and familiarity by such a modern-looking restroom so far from home, you don't even think to check to see if there is any toilet paper in the stall.

That's because in America there are always several giant-sized rolls in industrial-looking acrylic dispensers. That's the problem: your eyes are fooled into thinking that there *must* be an adequate supply of toilet paper. Suddenly, you are in the middle of your business on a Chinese toilet when you realize with horror that there *is* no toilet paper. There may be one of those industrial-looking acrylic dispensers, but it is empty.

The reason is, of course, so obvious that only a Westerner would fail to understand the logic. If the Chinese provided free toilet paper, what are the chances that someone, sitting out of sight in the stall, would pull out, say, a hundred feet of toilet paper from a giant-sized roll and simply carry it home for later use? Obviously, they see the likelihood as very high. The truth is that paper products don't come cheap in China, even if you are a typical worker. The things that we all take for granted are thought of differently.

Now, don't get us wrong: the smaller airports and places like the fancy new malls *do* indeed provide toilet paper, but it's in the logical place—OUTSIDE the toilet stalls, right inside the entrance to the restroom! Any Chinese person knows that, upon entering, you simply need to grab a few pieces of what looks and feels like thin, coarse crepe paper and take it with you into the stall. Better still, you are wise enough to bring your own supply of toilet paper in your purse.

Qin has had the experience of being in a restroom at the Capital City Airport in Beijing in 2005, before the expansion and renovations in 2007–2008, when she heard a pathetic cry for help from one of the stalls. The woman was frantically yelling, "There is no toilet paper! Please help me!" Qin could see her desperate expression because the woman had actually opened the door to her stall to beg for help. There were at least fifteen people in the restroom, plus the female attendant, but no one offered any assistance. Not one to leave a fellow human being in such a pitiful state, Qin hurried to the entrance where the big toilet paper holder for the entire washroom was located. She grabbed a handful of toilet tissue and handed it to the woman.

As far as the men's restrooms are concerned, the same rules apply, that is, should one need to sit. The main difference, however, relates to the ubiquitous male attendant lurking around in the washroom. After you have visited the urinal or stall and made your way to the row of sinks to wash your hands, you will notice this "official-looking" attendant approaching you and offering you, from his pocket, what looks like a towel for you to dry your hands. There are several reasons why we suggest you do not take advantage of what seems a considerate and selfless act:

- The so-called "towel" is really thin tissue of dubious origin.
- The paper is so thin it literally falls apart in your hands.
- If you look around the restroom, you'll notice that even though there are no paper towels, there is an electric hand dryer attached to the wall that you can use for free.

- Most importantly, if you do accept the gesture of service the attendant offers you, he will then expect that you will tip him accordingly.

In the most famous tourist sites frequented by foreign tourists there are an increasing number of restrooms that are up to Western standards, with sit-down toilets and all necessary toilet items provided. However, if you plan on doing a lot of sightseeing even a little off the beaten track, know that most public restrooms in China do not provide toilet paper at all. Chinese people know to always carry their own supply. It's a good idea to keep a small supply with you at all times. You can take a roll along from your hotel room if you have room to carry it. Be aware, though, that Chinese hotels are very stingy in usually giving you only one or two very small rolls. If you want to buy your own supply on the street, it is quite easy to find small "convenience-store" type shops that sell all manner of bathroom supplies and toiletries.

Most public restrooms in China do not provide you with soap either. They also rarely offer hot water from the tap. You will need to bring your own supply of "wet wipes" or a bottle of hand sanitizer to use throughout the day. Many public restrooms in China do not provide either paper towels or a hand dryer, although a lot more of them provide a dryer than provide toilet paper or soap! It's not a bad idea to carry a handkerchief with you to dry your hands. Many public toilets in China are still of the infamous "squat" variety, though in recent years there has been a marked increase in "sit-down" Western-style toilets. The aptly named "squatty-potties," as we affectionately call them, require that you squat on your haunches over a hole in the floor. Keep in mind that many of these toilets are of the flush variety—it's not like a port-a-potty at the state fair. If you're lucky, there will be porcelain inlay on either side of the hole. This is where your feet should go.

The "squatty-potties" have never found favor in the West, which is strange since they do have a practical advantage over the toilets we're used to. Since your bottom doesn't actually touch a place touched by the bottoms of countless other people, the hygienic issue for the most part is a non-starter. The vast majority of Chinese people prefer this kind of toilet for this very reason, even when given the choice between squatting and sitting on a toilet seat. Since toilet seat covers are considered a useless luxury and your supply of toilet paper is already limited, you also don't have to worry about covering the seat before you sit down if you were using a Western toilet. Given the fact that there is usually no air-conditioning in public restrooms in China, the inside of a restroom often resembles a sauna. If you do cover a Western-style toilet seat with toilet paper, upon arising when the deed is done you will find that all the aforementioned paper is now stuck to your rear.

The main problem with the "squatty-potties," and it *is* a big problem, is that they simply have not found a place in the Western *aesthetic de toilette*. In China, where things are usually slow to change, this can mean a long, fruitless search for a familiar-looking toilet. In many public restrooms in China there is no choice: all the stalls for men and women are of the squat variety. The nicer the restaurant or the more famous the historical site, temple, or museum you visit, the more likely it is that the restroom will have a Western-style toilet somewhere behind one of the many stall doors. Increasingly there are pictures on the stall doors indicating the type of toilet you'll find inside. Our advice is to not immediately get discouraged upon opening the stall door to find a "squatty-potty." Do not give up until you've tried every stall in your quest for a pleasant experience. However, don't be surprised if your joy at discovering a sit-down toilet is somewhat dampened by the fact that the previous Chinese occupant has squatted on the toilet seat, leaving shoe prints on it as a memento of her visit.

To avoid having to use the toilet more than you normally do, be sure to take with you a fair amount of Imodium A-D. Standards of hygiene in China are not as high as in the West. Our bodies have also not developed a resistance to the bacteria common in China. If you eat at the better restaurants in the major cities, you likely will experience no digestive issues. But should you be struck by what we call Mao Zedong's Revenge, you will want to avoid spending valuable sightseeing time getting all too familiar with Chinese toilets!

2
Never Take a Black Cab and Other Taxi Tips

Having used the restroom, you retrieve your luggage from the very modern and up-to-date baggage carousel in the airport. You've been cleared through immigration and customs and you're now ready to take a taxi into town. This will be the first of many taxi rides you will probably take in China. As we'll talk about later, many Chinese are just itching to take a foreigner, literally and figuratively, for "a ride." Taxis are everywhere. There are around sixty thousand in Beijing alone and thirty or forty thousand in Shanghai. Taxis are also much cheaper than in America.

You will probably take a taxi from the airport to your hotel, just as you will likely be taking taxis to get around in the cities. There are plenty of public buses, but most are filled with locals packed in like sardines. It is a unique experience for most foreigners to be in a bus pressed in so tightly by other human bodies that you feel yourself lifted off your feet. Major cities do have subway systems, as we discuss in the next chapter. The ones in Beijing and Shanghai, among others, are an excellent and extremely cheap way to get around town. But often a subway station is a bit far from where you are or the subway may not run very close to your destination. Subways also require a bit of a hike to get to the trains, even after you've reached your station. So you'll find that taxis are a tempting way to get around, particularly because they're so ubiquitous and so inexpensive by Western standards.

You can hail a taxi on any well-traveled street in any Chinese city. In the busier sections of cities like Shanghai we've stood on a street corner and counted as many as thirty taxis pass us by in the space of exactly sixty seconds.

The cabs in Beijing all charge 13 yuan for the first 3 kilometers and 2.3 yuan for every subsequent kilometer; charges are similar in Shanghai, and in smaller cities the fare will be lower. The general rule is, the smaller the city, the cheaper the fares. In the city of Yangzhou, with a population of 4.5 million compared to 27 and 25 million for Shanghai and Beijing respectively, the charge for the first 3 kilometers is only 7 yuan, nearly half the price in Beijing.

All taxis these days have air-conditioning. Just make sure the driver turns it on. He might be trying to save gas by leaving it off and rolling down the windows instead. This is commendable in that it helps conserve a precious natural resource and cuts down on pollution. Politely utter the magic words "kōngtiáo" (pronounced "kung tee-ow") or "qǐng kāi lěngqì)" (pronounced "ching kai lung chee)," meaning "please turn on the air-conditioning," and the driver will usually oblige. On longer trips, be sure to take down the number of your taxi so you can report the driver if he "takes you for a ride" or if you leave something valuable in the cab that you need to retrieve. Do not assume you're being cheated, however, if the taxi driver asks you for

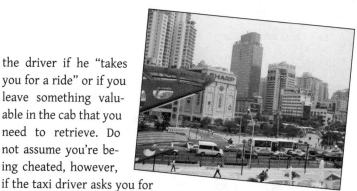

several yuan more than the price on the meter. In recent years taxis have added a fuel surcharge (what is called the "Beijing Taxi Special Invoice Of Bunker Adjustment Factor"!). So if the meter says 20 yuan, for example, get ready to pay 22 or 23 yuan. Also be aware that taxi fares in cities like Beijing and Shanghai are a bit more expensive late at night than during the day. Of course, like most things in China, everything is in flux. These policies could change any time!

Just as with most Western airports, the taxi stand is right outside the airport arrival hall doors. On your way to lining up at the official taxi stand you very likely will be approached by a friendly man or woman who will offer you a ride into town. This person may even be wearing an official-looking tag identifying him or her as an employee of the airport. You assume that this is a taxi driver and that if you take his or her car you can save precious minutes waiting in line. This would be a bad decision. This man most likely is the driver of a "hei che" (pronounced "hay-chuh") or, literally, "black car." By "black" the Chinese mean "dark," "nefarious," and, therefore, "illegal." As if to live up to their name, the cars these drivers use were generally black, to avoid attention, a direct contrast to the colorful, eye-catching look we've come to associate with taxis worldwide. Now they could be any color, though. The drivers of the "black cars" have not paid the money for a taxi license and belong to no taxi company. That means their car will have no meter and they will charge you whatever they like for the ride. Some tourists have been told when finally reaching their hotel after a circuitous "scenic route" that they owed thousands of yuan. Usually you end up paying 200 to 300 yuan for a ride in a "black car" instead of the 110 to 120 yuan you'd pay for a real taxi. Ignore all offers of a ride and wait in line at the cabstand. Just follow the crowd. Another advantage of standing in line at the cabstand are the government workers standing there to direct you to a cab, so there is little chance you'll be cheated on the fare. However, you should still write down the number of the cab and the driver who will be taking you into the city, just in case you have any complaint or leave anything in the taxi, you'll have some recourse.

Whenever you take a taxi anywhere in China, whether you're heading to a hotel, a restaurant, or a tourist site, have the address and telephone number of your destination written down for you in Chinese to show the cab driver. The staff at the front desk of your hotel will be happy to do this for you. If you're going from your hotel, you can always ask the doorman of a four- or five-star hotel to call a cab for you. Tell him your destination, and he will inform the driver. Especially if you're taking a cab from somewhere other than your hotel, it's always a safe bet to have the information about your destination written down. At the front desk of your hotel you can obtain a card with the hotel's address; always carry this card to show the cab driver when you're returning to your lodging.

If you're heading to a major hotel or tourist site, to the airport or the train station, the driver will undoubtedly know where to go. If you are headed to a lesser-known place, the driver can use his cell phone to call and get directions. Even in Beijing, an increasing number of cab drivers are not originally from the city and do not know the geography as well as taxi drivers in the past. Best to have the information about the place you're going written down in Chinese.

Now might be a good time to discuss tipping in China. The good news is that it isn't the custom to tip for most of the services you'll receive. That includes taxi rides. Taxi drivers in the U.S. need the promise of a tip to give them the incentive to drive you quickly and safely to your destination. The Chinese cab driver needs no other reward beyond the fee on the meter . . . and, of course, the great delight in watching through the rear-view mirror the panic-stricken look on the face of the foreign tourist as the cab weaves in and out of lanes at breakneck speed, defying death at every turn. In recent years a large number of Chinese people, including the elderly, have come to depend on taxis as a reasonably priced and easy way to get around. If foreigners tip cabbies so that they come to expect it, cabs will become pricier for locals. When a Western traveler offers to let the cabby

"keep the change" when paying, the driver very likely will be confused as to your intention. The rare exceptions may be when taking a cab to or from the airports in Shanghai, where the driver may not offer to give you change if it's just a matter of 10 yuan or less. They may simply pocket the money and drive off. This is because these drivers have gotten accustomed to serving foreigners who have tipped them in the past.

Tipping is also not customary in restaurants. Unlike the U.S., where we need to tip "to ensure promptness and good service," most countries in the world automatically add the tip to the bill. In fancier restaurants in China a gratuity of 15% is routinely added.

There are times when a tip is expected in China. The porters in the hotels expect a tip of 10 yuan (a little over a dollar) for helping you up to your room with your bags. Unlike in the U.S., however, if you fail to tip them they will simply leave the room. They won't stand there with their palm up explaining every feature of your room until you pay them to stop, as is the custom in America.

One major exception to the rule about tipping is that if you hire your own personal guide and driver, as some of us do in more remote areas of China, you will be expected to tip both of them at the end of their time with you. That's because these people are used to serving only foreign tourists. They know all too well our American custom and think it's a dandy idea. The general rule of thumb is that you give 100 yuan (about US$15) to the guide and 50 yuan (about $7.50) to the driver for each day they served you. It would be nicest if you took some envelopes from the desk in your hotel room to put the money before presenting it to them when you say goodbye.

3

Subways
(Fast Trains, Not Fast Food!)

Taxis are certainly a convenient and quite inexpensive way to get around in Chinese cities. But in Beijing, Shanghai, Guangzhou, and twenty-five other cities, a fairly new and excellent alternative has emerged in recent years, namely the subway. Although taxis are much cheaper than in the U.S., even in the largest cities in China, the roads are increasingly congested. There are five million vehicles in Beijing alone, with more on the road every day. At peak traffic hours you may discover that your cab is only creeping along toward your destination. It may not move forward at all for minutes at a stretch. With that in mind, you might want to consider taking the subway in Beijing and Shanghai. The number of subway lines has greatly increased just in the last few years, making the subway a very viable alternative to taxis. It's safe, really cheap, and often much faster than taking a cab. It's also the environmentally correct thing to do. The subway cars are new, clean, and air-conditioned in the summer. You'll also get to mingle with Chinese people, LOTS of them. In Beijing it only costs 2 yuan (about US30 cents) for an entire day of travel, including unlimited transfers. In Shanghai the price is

3 yuan (about 45 cents), but when you transfer, you'll need to go to the ticket counter to pay an extra yuan (about 15 cents) for each transfer.

The names of the stops are written in romanized Chinese for foreigners, as well as in Chinese characters, both in the subway stations and on the maps inside the subway cars. There are also announcements made clearly in both English and Chinese before each stop, as well as a flashing sign above the door at each end of your car that will show the name of the station you're approaching. There are automatic vending machines to buy the tickets for your destination, into which you can insert either paper money or coins.

If you're staying in a city like Beijing for any length of time, buy a multi-use card for 30 yuan (US$5). This card, called 一卡通 ("yìkǎtōng"; pronounced "ee-kah-tung"), will allow you to take any subway line or ride any bus by simply swiping your card at the turnstile at train stations or when boarding a bus. A 30-yuan card should be sufficient for lots of rides over four or five days.

Should you have trouble using the machines, there will always be station employees there who will quickly step in to help the perplexed foreigner. In some smaller stations there are booths with a person to sell you the tickets. In any case, this is China, so there are always people around to help you.

After you've bought your tickets but before going through the turnstiles, you'll need to go through a security checkpoint with a conveyor belt, on which to place the larger items you're carrying, and a scanner, just like in an airport. In fact, you'll need to go through the same kind of security check when you enter almost any train station, when you board a boat, or when you enter stadiums, museums, or auditoriums for theater plays, and even when entering a national park! The same restrictions as in airports about bringing liquids with you seem to apply, although the security personnel will usually allow you to take your own beverages through as long as you take a swig to prove it's legit.

When you are ready to pass through the turnstile to go to your track, run your ticket or card over the scanner at the top of your turnstile and the little gate will open. Be sure to keep your ticket, because you'll need to feed it into the turnstile when you arrive at your destination and exit the subway station.

The subways can be very crowded, of course. You also have to be prepared that people will not line up in an orderly fashion here. Nor will the people getting on the subway at a stop necessarily wait for you to get off before they rush aboard. So you'll need to be politely assertive. But for all this, if you take the subway, you'll certainly save money and probably save time. You'll also feel good that you have reduced your carbon footprint by refraining from taking a cab.

4
How to Stand in Line and Not Have a Cow

As the Chinese themselves will constantly tell you: "China has too many people!" It's a daily mantra repeated by all Chinese, from taxi drivers to university professors. For some reason, and we're not sure exactly why, the vast majority of China's population have never learned the concept of lining up in an orderly fashion. Unless you see it for yourself you simply won't believe it. People in Western countries generally consider the law of "queuing up" absolute, and woe to anyone who thinks otherwise. So do the Japanese, for that matter. Even in Hong Kong, proud former British colony that it is, the locals (who, let's face it, have been known more for their pursuit of wealth than their people-friendly skills) still look down with scorn at their "backward" country cousins across the border who seemingly don't know the meaning of lining up in an orderly way.

Perhaps it's because Chinese people have always had two sets of rules when it comes to how to treat others. They treat their friends and family with the greatest care and concern. They treat strangers with total indifference, and courtesy goes out the window. Or perhaps it's because there are just too many

people wanting the same goods and services. The feeling is that if you don't push and shove to make it to the head of the line, you'll probably have to wait all day for what you want. And it doesn't help that for the first thirty years of Communist rule, there was no concern with etiquette or manners. It was a society that took pride in attacking anyone and anything that was refined. Refined manners, after all, belonged to the former ruling class of aristocrats and scholars.

In any case, never näively think that you can just line up behind the folks ahead of you, secure in the knowledge that the people behind you will courteously *stay* behind you. You will soon discover that not just one person but often a number of them will try to get ahead of you in line. Even if you leave just a foot of space between you and the person in front, you'll often find that somehow or other a person has rushed in from parts unknown and managed to squeeze himself or herself into that foot of space. So get close to the person standing in front of you in line. Real close. Close enough to see if they shampooed this morning.

The caveat here is to use your best judgment when in a situation like this. Try to blend in and don't make a scene. Don't yell or rant. It sometimes seems as if watching foreigners crack under the relentless pressure of Chinese society is a favorite pastime among the locals. It doesn't matter whether you are waiting for a taxi at the airport, queuing up at an airline counter, buying tickets of any kind, or checking in or out of a hotel. There is a fine line between blending in and doing as the locals do, and becoming so frustrated with it all that becoming an Ugly American seems like the only way to get anything done. The only places where people are really forced to stand in line and obey the queue are the areas where people wait for taxis at the Beijing and Shanghai Airports. In the past few years, the waiting crowd is forced to line up within the tightly cordoned-off areas. These are pretty much the only places where we have observed the Chinese faithfully wait their turn in a queue. Consider these taxi stands as special places of courtesy and order in a country where respecting the queue still seems a foreign concept.

5

What to Expect (and Inspect) at Your Hotel

China now has a large number of four- and five-star hotels in all the major tourist locations. You will have no trouble finding a very comfortable place to stay in the Middle Kingdom, although these days the prices can be almost as high as for an equivalent hotel in the U.S. In addition to the recognized Western chain hotels, there are numerous domestic hotels, catering mainly to a Chinese clientele. The latter can be a bargain if you know what to look for. Remember, of course, that what is called a five-star hotel in China would only be rated as probably a three- or four-star hotel in America; a four-star hotel in China would only garner two or three stars here, etc. If a hotel has a one-star rating, you are probably better off sleeping on the street. Nevertheless, finding a nice place to lay your tired body down in the land of the Great Wall should not be a problem.

Checking the Name of Your Hotel

If your local travel agency arranges your trip through a travel agency in China, which is the usual practice, make sure you don't just get the English name of your hotel. Get the Chinese name of the hotel as well, so you can show it to the driver, along with the correct address. The problem here is that the English and Chinese names of hotels are not literal translations of each other, and English names of a large number of hotels often bear little or no resemblance to the meaning of the Chinese name. While it's true that many taxi drivers in Beijing and Shanghai might know the names of the best-known hotels in English, do not count on that, especially outside of the very largest cities in China!

Checking in and Checking Your Room

Checking into a hotel in China is much like checking into a hotel in any other part of the world, except for one little thing. The friendly folks at the front desk will very politely and smilingly inform you that they require a deposit of from 200–500 yuan or more PER DAY, depending on whether it's a four-star or five-star establishment, but less than this for a two- or three-star place. They're very happy to welcome you, but your honest-looking face is insufficient to assure them that you won't be sneaking any towels or pillowcases or bottles of beer out of the room when you check out. You can pay the required deposit with either a credit card or with cash. Just make sure that when you check out, you get this money back. Also be aware that, unlike in most hotels in the U.S., you will be charged for each local phone call you may make. And you'll be charged for those local calls by the *minute*!

Once you arrive safely at your hotel and check-in, you figure you can finally relax now. You can't wait to unpack, shower, change clothes, and begin exploring. Wrong, wrong, wrong! First check carefully to see if everything in your room is in working order!

The biggest problem you encounter with Chinese hotel rooms, even if you're staying in a five-star hotel, is that very possibly something will be wrong with the room. It won't be something terribly serious, like having a hole in the wall, but something will be amiss, even if you don't notice it at first glance. And in every hotel it will be something different.

The reason something is probably not quite right with your room is that most buildings in China are put up very hastily and as cheaply as possible; they have to be in order to keep up with the incredible construction boom. This is a classic paradox: on the one hand, the building (or hotel room) will seem beautiful, but this is often a façade concealing shoddy construction and poor attention to detail. There is little concern for a little something we in America like to call QC, or "quality control." This is slowly changing, but because of shoddy design and workmanship, a hotel only five years old can (and often does) resemble something two decades old or more. Anything that can possibly break most likely will; either a switch will not operate or a latch won't work right. You need to check that everything is working, especially the basic things like the faucets and the toilet. Make sure that the sink and the shower doesn't leak and that the shower drain actually allows water to escape from the tub. Check that the air conditioner really puts out cold air. Look to see if there are washcloths in the bathroom.

Most Chinese staying in hotels aren't accustomed to using those handy little towels we Americans depend on to soap ourselves with, so Chinese hotels in smaller cities might

fail to put them out automatically for guests unless you ask for them. If there are no washcloths or anything else is missing, you can always call the number listed by the phone for "Housekeeping." Ask for "xiǎo fāngjīn" (pronounced "see-ow fahng-jin"), which is Chinese for "little square towel."

There is one good thing about Chinese hotels that have at least a four-star rating. The staff is quick to answer your call for help, since they expect there will be problems. It's likely they wait by the phone, crouched down in the position runners assume at the beginning of a race. They know that any minute the phone will ring with another complaint. And they're almost always really friendly and anxious to remedy the situation. In our experience the staff usually arrived within two minutes of our call. This is pretty impressive in light of the fact that we've stayed in around fifty hotels in China and probably made around a hundred calls for help!

While you're checking that everything in your hotel room is in working order, look for soap. Many Chinese hotels provide one tiny biscuit of soap for you to use in the sink. But for the bath they often provide a very small plastic bottle of liquid soap. Personally we consider these miniscule bottles of liquid soap a real pain, since all you can squeeze out onto your washcloth is a little dribble and it's hard to get a good lather going. If like us you would prefer to use a bar of soap in the shower, call "House-keeping" and say the magic word "xiāngzào" ("seeahng-dzow").

Below is a "small" list of some of the things that might be wrong with your room. We'll include the snafus mentioned above just so you'll have a complete list. We know from personal experience these things need to be checked, because the items below cover the problems we sometimes encountered in hotels during recent trips around China. We include these because they are all common problems in four-star hotels. You most likely won't have to worry in five-star places, but "to be forewarned is to be forearmed!"

- leak under the sink
- leak in the bathtub
- bathtub drain not working: Don't wait until you're tak-ing your first shower to find this out. You could be up to your armpits in water before you get all the shampoo out of your eyes!
- faucet in the sink keeps dripping, or even pouring out water
- air-conditioning not working (usually it's not plugged in)
- air-conditioning vent leaking water from condensation

- stink in the hallway from recent painting or other re-modeling work
- safe not working—either won't lock or won't open
- water boiler not working
- mini refrigerator not plugged in
- TV cable not connected, so no TV reception
- dead (or missing) batteries in TV remote control; not functional
- no light to read by: either some lights are burned out or the bulbs they put in are only ten or twenty watts
- not enough or no towels, washcloths, or soap

In fact, as soon as you enter your hotel room, you might be convinced that nothing works at all. You try to turn on the lights and—nothing happens. That's because you have to take your room key card and insert it in a slot near the door for anything electrical to work. In a nation like China where electrical power is at a premium, the hotel needs to make sure that you don't leave all the lights on in the room when you leave for the day. Europeans have learned the wisdom of this and use the same type of system in many of their hotels. We Americans, however, like the idea of returning to a hotel room that's all lit up, so everything will seem very homey and inviting when we get back from visiting the Great Wall. The Chinese just don't have electric power to burn, so to speak. So get used to inserting that key card before flicking any switches. In the very best hotels, when you take out the key card upon leaving the room, the air-conditioning

will stay on. That is not true, however, with less expensive hotels. In those cases you need to bring along an old plastic library card or something of that shape and size to leave in the slot when you go out, so that the air-conditioning will remain on while you're gone. That way in the summer months you won't be returning to a room that resembles a sauna, particularly in the steamy, sticky south of China. If you should stay in a four-star hotel in a smaller city, you may discover that, with or without the room key inserted, the air-conditioning will not come on until after 9:00 P.M.! Do not hesitate to ask for an electric fan ("diànshàn," pronounced "dee-en shahn").

The ubiquitous "bedside console" is legend in Chinese hotel room lore. A combination nightstand/reading table and "mission control" center for your room, there are numerous switches that can control (so it is said) the TV, radio, reading and room lights, alarm clock, etc. We've never found the consoles to work well, but if you like pushing buttons, they are a lot of fun.

There will likely be a hair dryer in your room, but you might not be able to find it. Not to panic. While they may be attached to the wall in the bathroom in plain view, there is a good chance you'll find it in a drawer in the bathroom or in a drawer in the bedroom. Finding the dryer may be a little like an Easter egg hunt, but you can pretty much count on it being there in a four- or five-star hotel. If you think about bringing your own hair dryer, either buy an adaptor for 220 volts or have a dryer with two voltage choices. But even then, you may very likely be unable to plug your appliance into the outlets in your bathroom. Whereas our Western plug outlets are in two vertical and parallel lines, most outlets in Chinese hotel bathrooms are either in a V formation or upside down V formation. However, almost always there will be at least one outlet in the bedroom into which you can plug Western appliances like your hair dryer.

A recurring problem we've had, even in the best hotels, has been the toilet clogging all too easily. This is because, in an admirable effort to conserve water, the toilets in Chinese hotels are set to flush with a minimum of water and water pressure. To help avoid your toilet getting clogged, use as little toilet paper as possible. Then when you flush, although there are two adjacent buttons above the water tank, one for #1 and the other for #2, hold down both buttons simultaneously for several seconds to produce the maximum water pressure. Should your toilet still fail to flush, call housekeeping or the front desk. Mention your room number and utter the following incantation: "Mǎtǒng dǔzhù le" ("ma-tung dew-ju luh"), i.e., "the toilet bowl is stopped up." Within a few minutes a plumber holding a plunger in a plastic bag will appear, always accompanied by a female staff member to oversee things. You might then be advised to not put any toilet paper in the toilet, but to deposit it in the waste basket instead. As this is too unsanitary for most Westerners to consider, use as little toilet paper as possible and avoid a late night visit from The Plunger Man.

Even if everything works perfectly in your hotel room, as it did for us in the five-star hotels in both Beijing and Shanghai during our latest visit, we did have a bit of a problem just entering the room. That is because when first trying to get into our room, we did not slide the key card slowly enough along the slot for the little light to turn green, signaling that you can turn the handle and open the door. You should also be aware that in some hotels in Beijing or Shanghai, once inside the elevators and the doors close, you or some other passenger may need to use the card key to activate the elevator before you can press the button for your floor. You'll need to slide the card key slowly along the vertical slot by the buttons for the floors to get the elevator to move. The reason for this is security, so that people not staying at the hotel cannot ascend to the guest rooms. We feel this to be an unnecessary nuisance. Nevertheless, to paraphrase the American Express slogan: "Your card key: Never leave your hotel 'home' without it!"

Drinking Water

When you travel it's essential to stay hydrated. Human beings can go for a long time without food, but we can't live for long without water. When you're traveling your body has to work harder to get used to new surroundings; you do a lot more walking and expend a lot more energy than you would ordinarily. In addition, most of us tend to do our traveling in China during the hot summer months, when almost all the large Chinese cities often see temperatures between 90 and 100 degrees, with very high humidity. When traveling in China or anywhere else in the world, carrying a supply of water around with you on each day's outing is absolutely essential.

The problem here is that in the great majority of countries in the world it is not safe to drink the tap water without boiling it first. China is one of those countries. NEVER DRINK THE TAP WATER IN ANY HOTEL IN CHINA or anywhere else in the country, for that matter. A large number of hotels provide you with two bottles of "mineral water" which is safe to drink. And it's free. However, many of us can finish the contents of these bottles in two or three gulps. Many hotels instead provide you with a small water cooler/heater that contains water they've boiled for you. After you use up that supply, which can perhaps fill four glasses, you can always refill it yourself with tap water and press the switch to boil the water in this little contraption. That's time consuming, however, and still doesn't give you a large "reservoir" of drinking water for your daily excursions outside of your hotel.

The good news is that the Chinese people all have the same problem you have with obtaining clean, safe drinking water. There are, therefore, countless small shops on almost every street in China where you can purchase large bottles of drinking water for a very reasonable price. There are many decent brands, but our personal favorite is called "Wa Ha Ha." The title is from a popular song and means "baby laughing." What better

name for bottled water than "Laughing Baby"? It calls up happy memories of those baths our mothers gave us as little children, when they poured water all over us and got shampoo in our eyes. Other reliable brands include "Nongfu" ("Farmer") and Kang Shifu (Master Kang). Of course, you can pay for the extra bottles of mineral water in your hotel room or in the hotel gift shop. But their prices are often 20–30 times what you'd pay "on the street." For example, a bottle of mineral water that would cost only 2 yuan (about US30 cents) at a supermarket (chāoshì) or convenience store a block or two from your hotel will cost you 68 yuan in your hotel room! And you can get a bottle of the same brand of water that's twice that size for only 2.6 yuan (about 35 cents)! This kind of price gouging in Chinese hotels makes our American hotel minibar prices seem like bargains in comparison!

And in China a small shop, convenience store, or small "supermarket" with water, toilet paper, and other daily necessities at rock-bottom prices is rarely more than a block away.

If you're buying water outside the hotel, however, it is crucial that you keep in mind the following rule: always buy water from a store. Never purchase water from some person just standing around on the street if they only have a small number of bottles spread out in front of them on a tarp, or even behind a small stand. Even if the water looks perfectly clear, it's very likely these people have simply filled some empty bottles with tap water and skillfully resealed them. We're not kidding. Friends of ours have gotten very sick drinking water they bought in this way while traveling.

In summer, China's high humidity and intense heat may cause you to perspire much more than usual. Sweating gets your electrolytes out of whack, which can cause a headache. So if you are traveling in summer, consider taking Gatorade powder with you (such as the lower calorie G2 version in individual packets). Replacing your electrolytes is easy with just a single bottle of water and the powder, twice a day at least. Parasols or light-colored umbrellas will prove very handy in protecting you from the blazing sun. They will help you perspire less and are cooler than hats. You can buy very colorful ones almost anywhere in China for only 25 yuan (around US$4). Also take a good pair of polarized sunglasses. Sunscreen will protect your skin, but since sunscreens products available in China are dubious as to their effectiveness as well as their ingredients, be sure to bring some from home.

For those of us enamored of diet (wútáng or sugarless) soda, the good news is that Diet Coke and Diet Pepsi are now available in some of the ubiquitous convenience stores in Beijing and Shanghai, at least, along with regular sodas. That's in part thanks to the rapidly increasing number of overweight Chinese people as a result of their recent economic boom. An ordinary-sized bottle of diet cola, while much more expensive than a large bottle of drinking water, will still only cost you US35 cents. So if you can't kick the cola habit while in China, there are alternatives to just plain drinking water. Don't expect the colas to taste exactly like what you're used to in the U.S., however! They have much more of a syrupy taste. But "when in Beijing, drink like the Beijingers," we always say!

The Breakfast Buffet

When you stay at any decent hotel in China, a buffet breakfast in the dining room is always included in the price of your room. That's because, although China has gotten civilized enough to have hundreds of McDonald's, Kentucky Fried Chickens, and even Starbucks, they are not yet so enlightened as to boast a Bob Evans or an International House of Pancakes. This leaves many of us without a decent place to go for eggs and ham, let alone pancakes. Answer: the "free" breakfast buffet.

At the time you check into your hotel you may be given coupons for each morning's meal. In other cases you need to use the small paper folder that holds your room key and which has your room number on it. They tell you that you can head to the dining room for breakfast any time between the hours of 6:30 and 10:00 A.M. So you get up the next morning and head down to breakfast at the reasonable time of 8:30. The young hostess at the entrance eyes you suspiciously as you approach. Obviously you're some freeloader who's wandered in having smelled something cooking. You smugly hand over your carefully guarded tickets or your room key folder to show you belong there after all but the hostess gives you a dirty look. Seems in your morning grogginess you've handed her two losing Lotto tickets by mistake. When you finally fish out the coveted meal coupons, she waves you in curtly. But it seems you're on your own when it comes to finding a table.

You figure you'll get your food first and then find a place to sit. So you head for the buffet tables. Then you notice the crowd of guests that look like a delegation from the United Nations.

There are tourists from every part of the world. You think you see other Americans but it turns out they speak Russian, or German. There are also more and more domestic tourists coming from other parts of China. It seems like they're all descending on the food like a swarm of locusts. Who can blame them after all that airline food? Like acrobats the diners are all balancing two or three plates in their hands, and if they could balance a plate on their head, they probably would. They scurry from place to place desperately seizing anything in sight. So you do the only rational thing. You join them.

The breakfast items are usually segregated into "Asian" and "Western" sections. The former will almost always feature several variations of the ever-popular rice gruel, cold cuts of seemingly unfamiliar meat, noodles, steamed dim sum, braised fish with black beans, and a host of other food items, some of which you may have never seen before.

The Western section is usually larger. There are typically cold cuts of seemingly unfamiliar meat, slices of cheese, a chafing dish of scrambled eggs, pancakes, potatoes or hash browns (or some variation thereof), sausage or bacon, and several kinds of toast and pastries. There is usually a good selection of fruit (some fresh, some canned) as well as a cereal bar for health conscious Europeans and Americans where one can even find their beloved muesli and Rice Krispies respectively.

You go over to a chafing dish labeled "Germany potatoes." English translation: "German-style potatoes." You lift the lid to take some and suddenly your heart skips a beat. It seems you've grown a third hand! Maybe it's something in the water in China! But sure enough there it is—a hand appearing in front of you helping itself to a generous portion of the potatoes before your tongs ever touch the tubers! It's every diner for themselves, it seems.

In any four- or five-star hotel in China there will invariably be an omelet chef, hidden in some corner of the dining room. Be sure to look around for him, because the Chinese really know how to prepare eggs, along with just about everything else. The young chef has a skillet in front of him and he holds a metal spatula in his hand. "Omelets!" you shout with glee over the din of the dining room and make a mad dash for eggs. Unfortunately, there are already five tourists ahead of you, all holding an empty plate in front of them. You recall the touching scene in the musical "Oliver" where the young boy holds out his porridge dish and with a pitiful voice mutters "Please, sir . . . I'd like some more." Ten minutes later, juggling several plates and a tiny bowl of cereal, you and your companion look for a place to sit. It's then that you notice that there are no empty tables!

Almost all the tour groups are scheduled to meet at 9:00 down in the lobby for their daily excursion and so everyone pours into the dining room between eight and nine each morning. Our advice: Get up at 5:30 or 6:00, when the Chinese do, and be the first foreigners down to breakfast. That way you'll have the first chance to grab the potatoes. Or wait until the veritable locust swarm is gone after 9:00 for a sure bet at a table. Of course all the melon slices and bananas might be gone too, but you'll be able to sit where you like.

Exchanging Money

Money may be the "root of all evil," but somehow it's hard to buy anything in China without it. The Chinese officially call their currency *renminbi* ("the people's currency"). You may know this as the "yuan." That's the word printed in romanization as well as in characters on Chinese money and is the word the Western media use. Your hotel in China gives you the chance to exchange money right in the lobby. The exchange rate you'll get will be no worse than what the banks offer. That's because often the hotels are providing a service on behalf of the banks, or the local bank will actually set up shop inside the hotel for this purpose. When changing money there's a point when shopping

around for the best rate becomes a ridiculous pursuit; there's no point worrying over a few tenths of a percentage point. You'll get pretty much the same rate no matter where you exchange your money. Up until 2005 the Chinese government for several decades artificially kept the exchange rate at 8.2 yuan per U.S. dollar. Because the Western countries for many years had accused the Chinese of purposely devaluing the yuan, the Chinese finally caved into foreign pressure and in June of 2005 agreed to a revaluation of the yuan. That has resulted in the official exchange rate of around 6.15 yuan to the dollar at the time this book was updated in 2013. With the usual commission you'll end up with a bit more than 6 yuan to the dollar. In June of 2010 the Chinese announced that for the first time in recent decades the yuan would no longer be pegged to the U.S. dollar. This means the exchange rate will change in the coming years, perhaps dramatically. Most likely we'll be getting less than 6 yuan to the dollar in the near future.

The big question we're all faced with when we travel is: cash or traveler's checks? Of course traveler's checks are safer to carry around, but cash is simpler. Whether you exchange traveler's checks or cash, you will have to show your passport. You do get a slightly better exchange rate with traveler's checks, but they deduct a bigger commission with the checks so you end up with pretty much the same amount of money either way.

The next big question is where should you exchange your money? Unless you're traveling with a tour group where transportation has already been arranged for you, you'll need Chinese currency to take a taxi. Your local bank will most likely allow you to exchange as much money in Chinese dollars as you'd like, if you give them a few days to order the money. The exchange rate is only minimally less than you'd get in China, and since most of us only need to exchange US$500 or less for the entire trip, this certainly is the easiest route to go. We have always waited until we arrived in China to exchange money, since we usually require as much as the equivalent of several thousand U.S. dollars for our longer trips. When exchanging this much money, the slightly higher exchange rate attainable in China is worth the wait. Fortunately, the major Chinese airports have exchange counters in the arrivals area, and they'll be able to handle a currency exchange very quickly and efficiently. The exchange rate is only very slightly less than what you'd get at your hotel, but there is also a 50-yuan (about US$8) service fee tacked on.

After that, the most convenient (and quickest) way to exchange money is at the front desk of your hotel. However, whether you exchange cash or traveler's checks, just realize that some hotels will not let you exchange more than $200 per transaction. You may, however, exchange money many times a day at the same hotel, just not all at once. Most major hotels in the largest cities, on the other hand, will let you exchange much more than $200 at a time, with some allowing you to convert as much as $2000 in one transaction. If you're going to exchange that much money, however, it's advisable to give the Exchange Desk in the lobby twenty-four-hour prior notice of your request, to ensure that they will have sufficient funds on hand.

Some hotels will also not accept traveler's checks, only cash. Other hotels will let you exchange cash at any time, but have limited hours for exchanging traveler's checks, such as from 2:00 P.M. to 5:00 P.M.! You may always exchange either traveler's checks or cash at a bank, such as the Bank of China, ICBC Banks, branches of the Bank of Communications (Jiaotong Yinhang) as well as Bank of Construction (Jianshe Yinhang) allow foreign currency exchange. It takes much longer to exchange money at a bank than at your hotel, but at least it's orderly. Be sure to take a number as you enter the door and watch for your number to come up above the tellers' windows. Be warned, however. It often takes so much time to transact any business in a bank, and the Chinese people are constantly complaining to the government about it. For the sake of convenience, it is definitely better to exchange your money at your hotel. Unlike Europe or Hong Kong, there are unfortunately no money exchange centers on the street in China.

If you do decide to bring cash to exchange for Chinese money, make sure you get the bank in your country to give you nice, crisp, new-looking bills. On one of our recent trips we had gotten mostly $50 and $100 bills from our bank in Michigan, thinking

that we would only need
to carry a small handful
of money that way and
the exchange would be
quicker. Neither the
teller at our bank nor
we cared that the bills
were a bit creased, but when

we went to exchange our $50 and $100 bills at the money exchange table of our four-star hotel in Xiamen (Fujian Province), we were told that they could not accept old bills like the ones we had.

This becomes especially important when we tell you that you'll mostly need cash to pay for things in China. Elegant restaurants or big department stores will accept credit cards, but China is still mostly a cash culture. Even many restaurants or stores that certainly look big and fancy enough to accept credit cards expect you to pay in cash. Meals are typically not expensive, and you may well find that paper money can go a long way.

Another thing to keep in mind is that if you use cash for your transactions (usually 100 yuan notes), more often than not the shopkeeper, taxi driver, or whoever you give your money to will hold the bill carefully up to the light, scrutinizing it to see if it's fake. Don't be embarrassed or take it as a personal insult that all Chinese automatically assume a foreigner would be an unwitting carrier of fake currency. While banks have more discreet

ways of checking a bill's authenticity, most people just want to play it safe.

If you're traveling only to the largest cities like Beijing and Shanghai, you don't need to bring U.S. currency. There are Bank of China ATMs with English menus everywhere that work fine and have many more security features than in the U.S. Even in small cities now there are ATMs that accept foreign bank cards or credit cards. Because this is China, however, if the ATM rejects your card you may need to use the cash deposit machine next to the ATM to make a withdrawal. If you plan on using a credit card for purchases as well as for withdrawing cash from an ATM, contact your card company to ask them to honor transactions made in China, giving them the dates you'll be there. Another problem with the ATM machine is that the words on the display, as well as all the buttons (with the exception of the numbers), are in Chinese. Most ATMs are now programmed to have instructions in English, but you may come upon one that does not. The machine may look familiar at first, but be sure you know what you're doing so you can avoid the embarrassment of inserting your card and then not knowing which button to push to get it back.

Our advice is to forget about ATMs outside of cities such as

Beijing, Shanghai, and Guangzhou. Use credit cards to pay for hotels, meals in fancier restaurants, and purchases of expensive souvenirs in stores, but take enough cash along to pay for everything else. You need RMB for just about everything, because the only places that definitely accept U.S. credit cards are hotels and large restaurants or restaurants used to serving foreign clientele. Get that cash the quickest and most convenient way, at the Exchange Counter of your hotel.

The good news is that as long as you keep your money along with your passport and other valuables in a money belt or fanny pack, it is still safer to carry around a lot of cash in China than it is in Europe or America. In China there are still not many purse-snatchers on motorbikes, such as we've seen in Italy, or teams of pickpockets who bump into you to take your money while you're distracted, such as we've experienced ourselves in Prague. Estimate the amount of money you'll need for admission fees to major attractions, meals in small restaurants, snacks and drinking water, taxis or buses, and small souvenir presents, and bring enough cash. Tourists in China run the gamut from the frugal, unshaven backpacker to the traveler who goes first class all the way. We've found that US$300 per week is more than enough for the average person, since things like food and taxis are still very inexpensive in China by Western standards.

Keeping Your Money Safe

Despite (or, perhaps, because of) its population, China is a very safe society when it comes to personal safety. You're more likely to be mugged in your own backyard in the U.S. than late at night on the streets of Beijing or Shanghai. Though many European countries have more pickpockets than China, you still need to be careful with your valuables, including your money as well as your passport and airplane tickets. Chinese criminals generally don't like to deal with foreigners, and certainly any kind of robbery or assault type crime is extremely rare. Of course, if you are stumbling drunk down the street with your wallet half hanging out of your back pocket, you may just be too good a target for a petty criminal to resist. For the most part, however, keep your wits about you and you'll be fine.

Fortunately, most four- and five-star hotels in China have a small safe in the room that you're free to use. It's carefully concealed in the closet or mounted directly inside the wall. If the safe is in working order, though, it's not a bad place to stash your most valuable things except for the cash you think you'll need for that day's adventure.

Laundry

When traveling, sooner or later you're going to be faced with the necessity of washing some of your clothes. There are a number of ways out of this dilemma, of course. It's cheap to buy new clothing in China, which is not surprising since most products in the garment industry are made there and exported to the West. A good idea is to use the laundry service at your hotel. This is sadly no longer the bargain it once was in the "good old days" of the 1980s.

To show you the range of prices, here are typical laundry prices at an average four-star hotel in a smaller city, followed by prices in a typical five-star hotel in cities like Beijing or Shanghai (all prices are approximate):

- dress shirt or blouse: 24 yuan (US$4.00); 30 yuan ($6.00)
- T-shirt/sport shirt: 22 yuan ($3.70); 25 yuan ($4.15)
- men's slacks: 24 yuan (($4.00); 30 yuan ($5.00)
- women's slacks: 30 yuan ($5.00); same
- dress: 32 yuan ($5.30); 35 yuan ($5.80)
- skirt: 20 yuan ($3.35); 25 yuan ($4.15)
- shorts: 20 yuan ($3.35); same
- underpants: 10 yuan ($1.65); same
- socks: 10 yuan ($1.65); same

Dry cleaning is also available for all items, at a slightly higher price.

Given such exorbitant prices for laundry in the five-star hotels in places like Beijing and Shanghai, which so many of us Western tourists frequent, my wife and I have opted to do our laundry ourselves. We either take along soap from home, or buy packets of laundry soap at the stores near our hotel for the equivalent of a few dimes U.S., or simply use the soap provided in the bathroom. After filling the bathroom sink with soapy water, we wash our clothes out by hand in the manner of our ancestors, then hang them up to dry on the clothesline found over the tub in most hotel baths as well as on the hangers provided. Even though we may be staying in a five-star hotel, we're not too

proud to make our room look like the proverbial "Chinese laundry" by placing the hangers holding the wet clothing up on the ledge above the windows. This way the clothing will dry out faster in the air as well as by the warmth of the sun.

Should you opt for convenience, however, and don't mind paying an extra few hundred dollars to have your laundry done for you, the hotel provides a bag for laundry and a form, in both English and Chinese, on which you list the number of each item you want washed. Supposedly you just leave that bag of dirty clothes in your room before you leave in the morning and you'll get it back in the evening on your return from that day's adventures, neatly folded and fresh-smelling.

So far this seems to differ little from the system that American hotels use for guests to get their laundry done. What is different in the Chinese case is that the employees in a Chinese hotel might attempt to inspect every piece of clothing with you present before the wash is done and then again after the wash is returned. They want to make sure that the number and type of item is exactly what you have put on the form. That is because these employees are personally responsible should a guest claim they put in a Ralph Lauren dress shirt and got back a laundered T-shirt with "Joe's Garage" on the back. So be prepared for the

Chinese hotel staff to dump out all your dirty clothes on your bed and check each item against the checklist you filled out, and then again check each laundered item with you when they return everything in the evening. You will agree, however, that this gives you a lovely half hour in which to get to know some very nice young Chinese people, with whom you can discuss in halting English such heady topics as the difference between a dress shirt and a sport shirt.

There is something to be said for this way of handling the laundry as opposed to the 1980s in China. At that time the hotel would provide you with a long explanation in very creative English that warned the guest that should your "count" of the number of items to be laundered differ from the hotel's "count," the hotel's "count" would be assumed by the hotel to be correct and not your "count," and they would charge you accordingly. So if you said you had five shirts, but the hotel counted 50 shirts, they would charge you for laundering 50 shirts.

One hotel we stayed at in southern China in the early 1980s had an explanation similar to that above, namely: "should your count differ from our count, then our count will be assumed to be correct and not your count." The only difference was, on the printed notice, they had inadvertently left out the letter "o" from "count."

Elevators

Elevators work the same all over the world. What's different about elevators in China is the set of rules for entering and exiting the elevators. If you're an American in China, you must learn a whole new set of elevator rules from those you operated under back home. In a city in the U.S., for instance, when an elevator arrives at a floor and the door opens, the people who are waiting for the elevator generally let the people who are getting off the elevator actually get off the elevator before entering the elevator themselves. There is also a sense of fair play among Americans that, while they generally do not stand in line for an elevator, whoever arrived in front of the elevator first deserves to get on the elevator first. In China you can just forget all of the above.

Dealing with elevators can be a frustrating experience, and, along with the seeming futility of standing in line, can (and occasionally does) bring out the worst in tourists unused to the social landscape. The incessant crowding, the seeming disregard for decorum and "proper" behavior, will soon have you playing the "Ugly American" card. Just relax and don't take it personally. Use your space and protect it. It's OK to push and jostle, but above all keep your cool and don't lose your temper.

Massage in the Hotels

Massage, a form of traditional Chinese medicine, has a long history and is all the rage in China. Everywhere you go there are places advertising almost every kind of massage therapy imaginable. Foot massage is still one of the most popular forms of massage, and you'll see signs everywhere for places that offer that kind of service. Almost all the hotels offer a large selection of massage choices, from full body massage of various kinds to different kinds of foot massage, and everything in between. Usually the hotel will have a "spa" or a designated space offering massage services. Most of the time it's a perfectly legitimate

service operated by experienced and trained professionals. If, however, you're offered massage in your room, you need to realize that in some smaller provincial cities there is a slippery slope between legitimate massage therapy and another kind of massage. For those of us seeking relief from a sore back or sore feet at the end of the tourist day, the "massage" they're really offering may not be what the doctor ordered . . . unless the doctor is Dr. Ruth! In many hotels, as soon as a Western man enters his hotel room at night, within a minute or two his phone will ring. He picks it up and hears the sweet voice of a young woman with a simple question: "Yào àn mó ma?" (Would you like a massage?). One can only assume that the mystery caller(s) are in cahoots with the front desk staff, and possibly even operate with their blessing. It happened to us even when we were together as a couple in a very respectable hotel in Shanghai. It was only when Larry mentioned the Chinese word for police (jǐngchá) that the caller finally hung up. This kind of thing is unlikely to happen in Beijing, however, where things are more tightly controlled.

Regardless of whatever you may be offered in your room, the authentic "medicinal foot bath and massage" is 100% legitimate and is a true balm to your tired dogs as well as to your spirit. This we highly recommend. Most Chinese hotels employ a small army of young women from the countryside who have been trained for a few weeks in how to take all the pain out of overworked feet and make them whole again. The young woman will first bathe your foot in a small tub of hot water into which she has placed different aromatic Chinese herbs. This is supposedly to relax and soothe your foot, helping it to heal with ancient, mountain herbal remedies perfected over centuries by Taoist monks in remote temples on distant mountains. More likely the real purpose is to make your foot odor less severe so that the masseuse can bear to get near it! After a few minutes of soaking in the piping hot medicinal soup, the masseuse will start massaging every part of your aching and overworked feet. After a few minutes, you realize that this is good for both your sole and your soul.

Staying in Touch

At some point during your travels around China, you'll find yourself missing your loved ones back home and wanting to share your adventures with them. You'll be tempted to call them from the telephone so conveniently located next to your bed in your hotel room. This would be a big mistake. As in hotels around the world, Chinese hotels also charge you a few U.S. dollars a minute to reach out and touch someone back in your home country.

With the money it would cost you to talk for several hours to a few of your friends and family members, you could almost afford to fly back home to see them!

There are several very good alternatives. One is to have your loved ones call you, using an international phone card. These are available now at a supermarket near you. The cheapest phone cards for calls to China are easily purchased online from any number of websites, including nobelcom.com and callingcards.com. We have found these to be reliable and secure sites. Within a few minutes of purchasing one of these phone cards online with a credit card, you will be sent an e-mail with the access number to call and your pin number. With these phone cards it costs a mere two or three cents a minute to call China from the United States, any day at any time. Just be sure your friends and family are aware of the time difference between North America and China. Since all of China is in one time zone even though the country is as wide and large as the U.S., and since China does not use daylight savings time, China is twelve hours later than Eastern Standard time from the first day of spring until the first day of fall, and is thirteen hours later from the first day of fall until the following first day of spring. If, for example, you call Beijing or Shanghai from San Francisco or Los Angeles at 8:00 P.M. on New Year's Eve, it will already be

noon of New Year's Day in China!

Another easy and relatively inexpensive way to stay in touch with your loved ones is by e-mail. If you've brought a laptop computer with you on your trip and you're staying in a five-star hotel in a major city, it's very possible they'll have a place to plug in your computer or even have wireless service. Short of that, almost every hotel in China these days has a Business Center on the first floor with broadband Internet access that you can use to send and read e-mail. The more expensive the hotel, the more they charge for one hour of use, although most hotels will pro-rate the charges by ten-minute or even one-minute increments. Here you can expect to pay between US$8 and $20 to use one of their computers for an hour.

For a far, far cheaper and more interesting alternative to getting Internet access, try one of the more than a hundred thousand Internet cafes, or "wǎngbā" (pronounced "wahng bah") located all over China. Here the rates are usually as cheap as 3 yuan to 8 yuan (US40 cents to $1) per hour. You'll find these kinds of Internet cafes or bars on main streets in every Chinese city and even in small towns that are major tourist places. We were delighted to find an Internet bar in the tiny town of Dali, nestled in the mountains of Yunnan Province not far from Tibet.

They had eight computers, and, after waiting a few minutes for a Chinese teenager to finish playing video games on one of them, we were able to check our e-mail back in Michigan for around 40 cents an hour. When you plunk down 3 yuan (around US40 cents), the average price for one hour, as a deposit, you'll be given a tiny slip of paper with a long number on it. That's the password you'll need to type into whichever computer you arbitrarily choose from the banks of computers, before you click on the icon for Internet Explorer or whatever other web browser they may use. And all the computers have Broadband connection to the Internet.

Thanks to the miracle of the Internet and e-mail, you can stay in touch with those you care about from most parts of the globe almost instantly. In China, more than five hundred million Chinese access the Internet, and millions of Chinese now own computers. A much larger number of Chinese take advantage of the cafes that make Internet use accessible and affordable. You'll notice that almost all the people using the computers are young Chinese in their late teens or early twenties. You'll also observe that almost none of them are sending e-mails or searching the Internet for news or information. Almost every single one of them, whether in Beijing or a small town, will be playing video games by the hour. Just remember that there are loved ones back home that are waiting to learn you're safe and to share your adventures, so don't be tempted to follow suit!

Contrary to popular belief in the West, while it is true that websites that discuss the Tiananmen Massacre or issues related to Taiwan and Tibet are blocked, you will have no problem in accessing most Western news sources online, should you wish to follow world news. Since these websites are in English, the Chinese government does not feel the need to block them; most Chinese are not proficient enough in English or interested enough in world news to seek them out.

As of this writing the *New York Times* is not accessible online, owing to a series they ran in 2013 that was critical of the accumulated wealth of China's leaders. But you can at least watch CNN International in rooms of four- and five-star hotels in Beijing and Shanghai. To the frustration of us Western travelers, however, in the past few years the Chinese government has blocked Facebook, Twitter, and YouTube. As recently as 2008 we would correspond with some of our Chinese acquaintances via Facebook. Now we have to wait until we get home to share pictures of our trip via that popular site. But reading and sending e-mails or viewing your local newspaper online is no problem and isunbelievably cheap, if you'll only venture outside of your hotel a bit.

There are some drawbacks, however, to using Internet cafes in China. Besides handing over a small deposit before using their computers, foreigners must also show their passports to the young people working there, who then take down your name and passport number. While this has always made us uncomfortable, to date we have suffered no ill consequences from this. However, for those of you concerned about identity theft or other possible nefarious uses of your personal information,

you may want to refrain from patronizing the Internet cafes in China. The other problem with using these places is that, although most of them are ventilated well enough, the air-conditioning in summer may be minimal and many of the young male patrons will be smoking continuously. Many of these establishments are also a bit shabby, with the upholstery of the chairs torn and the floor sticky with the remnants of former patrons' sugary drinks. Other places may be very nice, indeed. Of course if you don't like the look of a particular wǎngbā, you can always leave and go looking for a nicer one.

However, for those of you who aren't particularly adventurous or who don't wish to spend much time online while in China, you may just want to briefly use the computers in the comfortable and very clean setting of your hotel's Business Center. In smaller cities like Yangzhou or Jiujiang, or in resort places like Lushan, some five-star hotels may allow you to use their computers free of charge. To our surprise and delight, this was true in three of the hotels we stayed in on our most recent trip. It won't hurt to ask the staff at the front desk if they would kindly do the same for you, telling them that you need to e-mail family and friends back home.

And there's always the option of spending all your time

outside exploring and waiting to e-mail your friends and family upon your return!

While we're on the subject of communication and related technology, let us recommend that you take some translation software. One option is an iPad with an app for going back and forth between Chinese and English. The best apps allow the Chinese to write in traditional/simplified/pinyin to communicate back to you. (Learn to use the app before you go!) Simple phrases like "My room needs more toilet paper" or "The toilet is clogged" are important (and show how essential this software can be). To learn some of the most useful phrases in Chinese for your trip, refer to Chapter 17, "Learning Chinese."

Checking Out

You may think that checking out of your hotel will be a breeze, just like in hotels in the U.S. Surely you can simply use their Express Checkout and drop the key at the front desk when you're ready to depart. After all, you've stayed at the hotel for several days or more and established a very nice rapport with the staff there. However, there is usually no such thing as Express Checkout in a Chinese hotel. When you check out of a Chinese hotel, you must hand over your key(s) to the folks at the front desk, who will then ask you to wait a moment while they make a phone call. They're calling the Housekeeping staff, to have them enter your room to make sure you haven't pocketed their alarm clock or put one of their pillows into your suitcase. You may find this lack of trust in their guests to be insulting, but there it is.

There is nothing personal about this check of the room upon checkout. It's simply that there is a serious lack of trust between people in contemporary China.

When you check out, of course the front desk will also have the maids check the minibar, to assure themselves that every beer and sugary drink is in its rightful place inside the refrigerator. Like us, you may have used the small refrigerator to chill the mineral water, soda, or beer that you have purchased much more cheaply outside of the hotel. Since the hotel has usually filled the little fridge with their exorbitantly priced minibar drinks, you'll need to remove their beverages to make room for your much cheaper ones. Very possibly they are the exact same drinks, but purchased at a fraction of the hotel price. Just make sure that you put back every single minibar item into the refrigerator. The maids will often ignore even full bottles placed on top of the fridge or on the table, and only count the number of bottles inside. Avoid being told that you'll need to pay an extra 100 yuan or so for beverages you never consumed but only moved a few feet!

In any case, count on it taking from five to ten minutes to check out of your hotel, unless there's anyone ahead of you in line at the front desk. In that case, it'll take even longer! But consider the bright side of this long wait. You'll have time to think about your next destination and the grand adventure that awaits you there!

A Walker's Guide
to China's Streets

Hotels in China that accommodate foreigners tend to be not only very large, but also self-contained. Many foreigners who come to China on business rarely leave their hotel except for their scheduled business meetings. More than just providing you with a place to rest your weary head at night, large hotels in China offer a choice of restaurants, many small shops for souvenirs and daily necessities, a recreation center, a business center with computers and fax machines, and laundry service—everything to meet your daily needs. Of course if you really want to see what China is all about, you're going to eventually need to leave the hotel and venture out into the streets.

The Fun of Walking the Streets

The fun of walking around a Chinese city is that so much life takes place out on the streets. In a developed nation like the U.S., most life takes place behind closed doors. In a society steeped in history and tradition like China, much more happens right out in the open—that's simply the way it's been for centuries. For one thing, most Chinese still don't own a car. They walk or take a bicycle or a bus to where they need to go, instead of each being encased in their own little bubble, out of touch with other people. For another, Chinese homes and apartments are much smaller than those in developed countries. Activities like washing clothes or cleaning vegetables, reading the newspaper, or even brushing one's teeth are often done right out in public in full view of passersby.

One more big reason why so much of daily life can be glimpsed outdoors is that in China there have been as many as two hundred million people who left their homes in small towns or the countryside to try to make a better life in the large cities. That means there is a sizeable population in every major Chinese city without any fixed abode. They eat, play cards and chess, and carry on their daily lives totally on the streets. In addition, Chinese cities are a giant collection of a myriad small shops and vendors' stalls and eateries that are often right on the street or with their storefront totally open to the street. Beyond going to the major tourist sites in any Chinese city, it behooves any foreign tourist to wander the streets and see how the Chinese really live. It's a feast for the senses and a photographer's delight.

There are two problems that a foreigner faces, however, when walking the streets of a Chinese city that one does not encounter in a country like the U.S. Neither has to do with personal safety. As we keep insisting, you are much safer walking the streets of Beijing or Shanghai, even at midnight, than you are walking in midday in your hometown in the U.S., whether that town is New York City or Pella, Iowa. No one has a gun, the police are everywhere, albeit often undercover, and serious crime is still a fraction of what it is in America. No, the two problems you face are ones for which most Americans are unprepared.

People, People, Everywhere!

The first difficulty in walking down the street in China is the sea of humanity through which you must wade in order to get where you're going. Unless you spend a good deal of time in downtown Manhattan or Chicago, chances are you aren't used to walking much. And when you do walk, you're used to being able to walk pretty much as fast as you'd like. In a Chinese city you have to learn to slow your pace because there will always be hundreds of people in front of you, behind you, and alongside of you.

Imagine the most popular store in your hometown the day before Christmas, when shoppers are knocking each other over to get to grab last-minute presents for friends and family. Now picture the density of people at a hundred times that of the store on Christmas Eve. Finally multiply the number of people by ten thousand. Place them out on the main street of your hometown and imagine them all trying to get somewhere at the same time. You now have some idea of what it's like on a typical Chinese city street at almost any time of the day or night. You're just not going to get anywhere very fast. The only way for you and your companion to walk side by side is for you to do what the Chinese do, which is to hold each other tightly by the hand or, preferably, link arms.

The crowded streets of Chinese cities, however, are only a

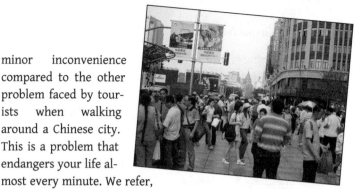

minor inconvenience compared to the other problem faced by tourists when walking around a Chinese city. This is a problem that endangers your life almost every minute. We refer, of course, to crossing the street. Here you are taking your life in your hands unless you realize that the Chinese operate under a completely different set of rules when it comes to things like "right of way." Crossing the street in China requires the watchfulness of an eagle, the agility of a mountain lion, the guile of a fox, and the luck of the Irish to make it across safely. If, however, you pay attention to the simple rules below, you may make it across the street and live to tell about it. Skip this section and you may end up spending the rest of your China trip learning more than you ever wanted to know about Chinese hospitals.

Crossing the Street

In the U.S. the pedestrian has the right of way. When the walk light comes on, the pedestrian may usually safely cross the street, checking briefly to see that all traffic has come to a halt. In China the pedestrian NEVER has the right of way. In fact, the right of way goes to the biggest and fastest vehicle. There's no written law that states this. Everyone just seems to understand. It's simple logic, really. Big trucks and buses take right of way over smaller buses, which lord it over taxis, which bully private cars. Taxis hold sway over other cars because owners of private autos don't want to damage their shiny new treasure, whereas most taxi drivers in China seem to have definite suicidal tendencies more akin to those of "kamikaze" pilots. Any motorized vehicle, including motorcycles, has the right of way over bicycles, whose riders will not hesitate to run over a pedestrian who dares question the vehicular pecking order by walking in front of them. While most vehicles do obey the stop and go lights, the millions of bicycle riders in China never worry about a little thing like a traffic light. Those, it seems, are just for cars and buses. Bicyclists may cross your path whether you have the walk light or not. The pedestrian is the low man or woman on the totem pole of Chinese traffic, the lowest link on the transportation evolutionary scale. Crossing a street is like playing a real life game of "Frogger."

How to cross the road when there are mad bicyclists coming at you from every direction and a constant stream of cars and buses? Learn from herds of wildebeests or antelope in the Serengeti. They know there is safety in numbers. Those that stray from the herd are the ones that usually end up getting eaten. So do what the Chinese do: Never cross the street alone, or even in pairs. Wait for a small group of local Chinese people who want to cross the street in the same direction you wish to go. Position yourself, if possible, in the middle of this pack of people. Watch for them to make their move and then go with them.

What can happen when a lone foreign pedestrian bravely

tries to cross the street on his own? Let us give you the sad example of Larry when he tried to lead the way across a street in downtown Shanghai at rush hour. Having located a crosswalk, albeit with no walk light, he started across the street, constantly looking left and right for oncoming vehicles. There was such a pile of cars and buses that traffic had come to a standstill. It seemed like an easy task to make it across. When he had reached the middle of the street, he turned and took a step back to beckon for Qin to follow him. Just then a young woman on a bicycle came out of nowhere and ran right over his foot. The bicyclist had precisely planned her move through the thick traffic based on Larry continuing to walk forward. But Larry crossed her up by turning back. He fell hard on the pavement, scraping both of his knees, which were bleeding profusely. Later that day he realized that his foot was broken and that it had to be set in a cast, which ended the trip a week early.

The Search for a Decent Toilet

While exploring whatever Chinese city you find yourself in, you will eventually need to relieve yourself. This is problematic enough in a developed nation like the U.S. It's a much greater problem in China, where there is such a startling disparity in the quality of restrooms. To find a clean bathroom that will have Western sit-down toilets, toilet paper, soap, and paper towels or a hand dryer, your best options are international-class hotels, fancy restaurants and bars, Western coffee houses like Starbucks and Costas (the U.K.'s answer to Starbucks), and upscale

shopping malls. Restrooms to avoid, if at all possible, include those in train stations (except those for the "G" bullet trains), subway stations, gas stations, outdoor markets, and public bathrooms on side streets, as well as those in tourist areas such as parks. These undesirable bathrooms will have none of the amenities that Westerners have come to expect and should only be used when absolutely necessary. Unfortunately, nature too often calls us at inopportune times. So whenever you're out and about always remember to bring a lot of toilet paper and wet towels such as Wet Ones or antibacterial lotion.

As in English, there are many different words in Chinese for "restroom." So the signs you need to look for when in search of a toilet will not always be the same. Although in airports and major train stations the signs will be in English as well as Chinese, or will feature a picture of male and female stick figures, in most places you will need to recognize the Chinese characters for restroom. The most common include 厕所 (pronounced "tsuh-swoh"), 洗手间 ("see-show-jee-n"), and 卫生间 ("way-shung-jee-n"). If you don't see any signs with those characters on them, then just go up to someone who works in that place, look pleadingly at them, and utter the words "tsuh-swoh" in a questioning manner. They're sure to point you in the right direction.

Should you be shouldering a heavy backpack and have a companion with you, leave the backpack with your companion before entering a stall in a public washroom. There most likely will be no hook in the stall for you to hang your backpack, or anything else. In the unlikely event that there is a hook there, it's usually just a flimsy thing made of plastic whose strength cannot be trusted. We have heard the alarmed cries from the occupants of other stalls when the heavy bag they had hung up caused the hook in the stall to break.

Queuing up for anything in China is always an issue, and that includes lining up to wait for a vacant stall in a washroom. You must not line up in the entrance area just in front of the stalls; if you do, others will simply walk past you to enter the next stall that opens up. They won't understand you're waiting in line, as the unwritten rules for this in China are different from those in the West. The Chinese generally stand in front of the door to a particular stall. Of course, if no one is standing in front of another stall that opens up, they make a bee line for it instead. So pick a door and stick by it to avoid having to make a mad rush to whatever door should open first.

Be aware that in many public restrooms there are one or two very steep steps you need to climb up just before you enter the stall. This is a nightmare for handicapped people, but can be hazardous even for the able-bodied. These ceramic-tiled steps are not marked with a different color than the floor or by any colored striping as a caution. Not only are these steps exceptionally high, but the bathroom floors are perpetually wet. Particu-

larly when exiting the stalls, keep in mind that these steps are right outside your stall door. Exit with great caution to avoid falling.

If you have no choice but to use an ordinary public restroom in China and you're wearing long pants, it's a good idea to roll up your pants before you enter. Most public washrooms are not sanitized with any disinfectant. Instead, those people who "clean" these washrooms only run a wet mop across the floor, which usually remains wet as well as unsanitary. Avoid having your pant legs touch the dirty water. Make like Tom Sawyer or Huck Finn and roll up your slacks.

Encountering Beggars

At this point remove your funny bone and set it aside. We need to talk a bit about begging and it's hard to find any humor in the misery of others. When you walk the streets of most countries in the world you will encounter beggars and in many developing countries you will sometimes be mobbed by them. Even in the U.S. we have people begging, and in a comparatively economically poorer nation like India or China you expect to see a lot more of it. When you consider how wealthy we Americans are compared to most people in the world, it's only natural that the impoverished in developing countries might expect us to toss a few coins their way. The problem is more and more people are thinking this way, and many Chinese cities have become magnets for a wave of human misery, and, sadly, those who profit from it. There is no point in ignoring it since you will not be able to avoid seeing these people on the street, but it's best to understand as much as you can before seeing any unpleasant surprises.

China is doing a whole lot better economically than most other developing nations. There has been a tremendous rise in the standard of living for a large percentage of Chinese in the past few decades. Part of China's economic miracle in the past thirty years is that the country has managed to move four hundred million people out of poverty and increased the average person's income more than eight-fold in less than one generation. Nevertheless, the average yearly income of a Chinese person today is still only around US$6,000 compared to around US$34,000 for the average American. But that's just the average Chinese income. There are huge, even staggering, gaps in wealth—stark reminders of China's free-for-all economy that is churning out more millionaires at a breakneck pace.

Since China has the greatest disparity of wealth of any nation now, a large number of Chinese live on the equivalent of only a few hundred U.S. dollars per year. Most Chinese do think of all Americans as wealthy. After all, we had the money to fly halfway around the world to make it to China, so you figure that at least some Chinese will view us foreign tourists as walking wallets and ask for a handout.

Actually, one of the impressive things about China is that, relatively speaking, there are so few people begging in the streets compared to most other developing nations. Most of the 1.3 billion Chinese people have adequate shelter, food, and clothing. You really won't be accosted in China by a great number of people begging. But they are there and you need to be prepared. Beggars in China may not be many, but there are quite a variety of them.

You might be approached by a young boy of five with a dirty face and tattered clothing, who will follow you around with his hand out. Or there might be an elderly woman who seizes you by the arm and won't let go, expecting you to give her money. Or you may see someone with his legs bent under him in shabby clothing sitting in the middle of the walkway with a cup in front of him, prostrating himself to passersby on a piece of cardboard.

It's not easy at first to pass these people by. Most of us have good hearts. It's also obvious how rich we are compared to them. The crippled people really pull at your heartstrings, and seeing children in such a state can be deeply troubling. What's even worse is that many children have been deliberately maimed or disfigured by adults, who realized that they can make more money by using a child to beg for them. As hard as it may be, do not give them money.

In front of our hotel in the heart of the city of Xian, for example, there is a relatively healthy-looking boy of around five or six years old whose daily job it is to work the front of the hotel. He approaches every foreign tourist with his palm out. If you ignore him, he will follow you for a distance tugging at your sleeve. Meanwhile his mother works a block or so down the

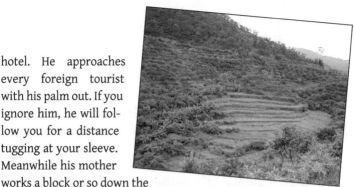

same street. Her job is to kneel in front of passersby with her youngest son and ask for money. But come noon, we have seen that mother gather up her two children and take them to Mc-Donald's. They are an attractive family, who look healthy and well fed. The only pitiful things about them are the smudged faces of the children and the dirtied clothing they wear.

For those who exploit children, making them do the begging work while they collect the proceeds, giving them money only makes the situation worse when you look at the big picture. It is hard to think of it in this way, but this is the reality. Try not to look at beggars or engage them in conversation. Rather, give them a wide berth when walking down the street. If one of them takes a hold of your arm, gently but firmly push it away and walk on with a determined gait. This is no time to practice speaking Chinese with the locals. Again, do not give them money, as hard as it may be. Give your money instead to an international charity or a local branch of a charity you know and can trust to help people who are in need.

Spitting in the Streets

Less than ideal sanitary conditions in China still make congestion of the lungs and throat an endemic problem for many Chinese. Another reason for all the coughing and hacking you hear may just have to do with the fact that over 60% of Chinese men smoke like chimneys. The traditional solution for getting rid of that nasty mucus build-up is by spitting it out on the street. This creates a number of little puddles that you will want to avoid. It's a bit like walking gingerly through a minefield, being careful to watch where you step. You must also keep your ears on the alert for the sound of someone about to "hawk." Much as the mosquito buzzes or the rattlesnake rattles before striking, the "hawker" first has to go into his wind-up before the pitch. The warning sound of someone collecting the phlegm in his throat is a lot like the sound "hur" as in the word "hurl." When you hear this sound, quickly move as far away as you can from the source of the sound. For men, if you are standing at a urinal and a Chinese man comes up to the urinal next to you, there is a 99% chance he is going to hawk and clear his throat, while taking care of business, in which case the sound will echo mercilessly off the bathroom walls.

If you can read Chinese, you know from your first day in China that spitting is a common phenomenon. Why else would there be signs everywhere telling you not to just spit on the streets as you please. In spite of the tremendous gains in literacy in China over the past few decades, somehow people don't seem to be able to read the characters for "spitting"! We'd suggest those characters be taught in the first grade!

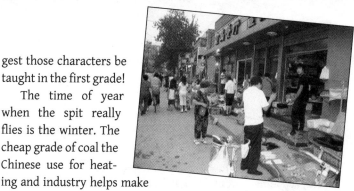

The time of year when the spit really flies is the winter. The cheap grade of coal the Chinese use for heating and industry helps make bronchial colds as common as sunburn at a nudist colony. If you're in China in the heat of summer, consider yourself lucky that the wetness you feel on your neck is only from your own perspiration!

If you had visited China several decades earlier, there would have been an additional kind of minefield you would have had to walk through on the streets. Those were the puddles left by toddlers who had relieved themselves as the need arose. Chinese tradition has always encouraged parents to wait longer to toilet train their young children than we do in America. Rather than putting a diaper on their youngster, Chinese parents will traditionally give them a pair of trousers with a slit down the middle. When the child feels the urge to go, he or she only needs to squat down and the pants will split wide open. For centuries this strategy worked just fine in the fields, where the youngsters would help fertilize the crops. On crowded city sidewalks, however, this isn't such a great idea. When the peasants started streaming into the cities in the early 1980s seeking a better life, it took a while for them to be convinced that the split pants were not welcome in downtown Beijing or Shanghai.

Hardships for the Handicapped

If an ordinary tourist feels handicapped by so many obstacles on a Chinese street, it is even harder for truly handicapped people. As in most developing countries, there are still too few places with accommodations for the disabled. There is too little public money and too little awareness to build such facilities. In museums, palaces, parks, temples, churches, etc., there are rarely any ramps for wheelchairs, for example. In addition, Chinese architectural tradition dictates the necessity of very high thresholds that you must walk over to enter any home or temple. This high threshold is to prevent evil spirits from entering. It also proves a true barrier for the handicapped. Add to that the Chinese predilection for long stone staircases leading to the inner sanctum of ancient temples as well as up the hillsides to even reach the temples, and you have a truly difficult scenario for anyone getting around in a wheelchair.

Public restrooms never make provisions for the handicapped. In many airport washrooms, for example, there are not one but two steps up to enter the stalls! For all these reasons it is rare to see any handicapped Chinese people venture out to many historic sites.

There is one more obstacle for handicapped and non-handicapped people alike that you should be forewarned about. This is the very common practice in most Chinese hotels of build-

ing the bathroom a half step lower than the rest of the hotel room. This means that you must always be prepared to step down into the washroom. Foreign tourists who are used to hotel bathrooms and bedrooms being on the same level are almost always surprised when they take that first step.

Essentials for Walking

Besides carrying some water with you as you wander through the streets of a Chinese city, it is highly suggested that you also have with you at all times the following equipment: earplugs.

Earplugs will be necessary to defend yourself from all the noise pollution you will encounter in a typical Chinese city. There is, of course, the constant stream of traffic that is a wondrous mix of buses, trucks, cars, taxis, motorcycles, and sometimes donkey-drawn carts. All of these vehicles, except the donkey carts, are equipped with horns. The Chinese driver would not be able to drive without constantly sounding the horn. It seems that in the driver's training manual in China the words for "clutch" and "horn" were inadvertently switched. The constant sounding of the horn by the Chinese driver alerts the thousands of people around him that he's in the vicinity and they better get out of his way if they know what's good for them. Unfor-

tunately, since everyone is trying to pass everyone else ALL the time, everyone is always sounding his horn. We recommend industrial-strength earplugs with a minimal rating of a hundred decibels. Then let the horns blare away.

Another reason for the earplugs is the quaint Chinese custom regarding garbage trucks. In China there are a lot of people. Those people produce a lot of garbage. Someone needs to be constantly removing that garbage. So the trucks come around at all hours to pick up the trash in the different neighborhoods. There's no place for dumpsters in most of China. The store and restaurant owners in shopping areas, for instance, have to bring their trash out to the truck when it drives by. In order to alert everyone to the fact that the garbage truck has arrived, the trucks are programmed to play a tune very loudly to announce their presence. It's a lot like the Good Humor ice cream truck that still comes to our suburban neighborhood in Michigan. But instead of carrying a yummy chocolate fudge bar, it's there to pick up your trash. And instead of playing something really rousing and lovely, like "Popeye the Sailorman," it plays something really annoying like "Rubber Ducky!"

Right in front of our hotel in the picturesque ancient mountain village of Dali, a garbage truck came by every day in the late afternoon to serenade us with "Happy Birthday to You" over and over and over again. The truck usually stayed there for five very slow minutes, blaring out "Happy Birthday to You" as if it were the Chinese National Anthem and this was "National Day" in China. Without earplugs we would surely have strangled the driver. Our earplugs definitely kept us from being involved in an international incident that would have included some major jail time.

If you intend to go to one of the many spectacularly scenic mountain areas where the elevation is more than a mile above sea level, you may seriously want to think about supplementary oxygen, as crazy as it may sound. You may not actually need to carry it, but it pays to know where you can get it. When we traveled recently to the high mountains of Sichuan, near the border with Tibet, Qin suddenly felt a shortness of breath. Now Qin has yet to reach the age that the Chinese call "half a hundred." She's also slim and walks many miles a day back in her adopted homeland of Michigan. But there she was, having trouble just taking a breath. Larry rushed to the local hospital where he was given an oxygen pillow with a breathing tube attached. This served as Qin's lifeline for the next several days.

The Public Parks

One of the most charming things about the cities in China is the great variety of activities to be enjoyed in the public parks. Besides being green spaces of beauty and tranquility, China's parks offer sights not frequently seen in city parks in other parts of the world. If you go fairly early in the morning, you will see large groups of senior citizens doing taijichuan (mispronounced in the West as "taichi"). Some groups will be holding fans while going through the movements of this ancient martial art. Another group might be holding decorative swords. Through much of the day you will likely see large groups of middle-aged people as well as retired folks doing ballroom or disco dancing to the music of a large boom-box. Very possibly there will be older men sitting beneath the cages of the songbirds they have brought from their homes, so that both they and their birds can enjoy the fresh air of the parks. Often there will be a group of senior citizens making music together, either on traditional Chinese instruments or singing traditional songs. There will certainly be people playing chess or cards, or getting a massage. Usually there is a lake somewhere in the park where you can rent foot-pedaled boats. While you're in China, try to spend at least part of one morning visiting a park. You might even consider joining in the dancing. The Chinese love to have foreigners join them, and you will feel most welcome.

7

Shop till You Drop

When visiting any major tourist attraction in China, you will need to run the gauntlet of numerous street vendors. These appear to have been ingeniously set up and placed in strategic locations for the sole purpose of enticing foreign shoppers.

Many of these vendors have stalls set up on either side of the narrow street leading to a famous temple or historic site. These professional salespeople are selling every conceivable kind of souvenir, from painted fans and painted scrolls to battery-powered pandas and Tibetan hats. They appear to be under strict instructions from the government to not allow any tourists to pass without trying to get them to enter their open-air shop. As you walk by you will be assailed with cries of "haroo, haroo" or "just looking, just looking." Somehow they have picked up on English-speaking tourists insisting that they were "just looking," and have twisted it around to mean "come in for a look and spend a pleasant hour or two admiring our merchandise." Should you stop to gaze at some picture postcards or a fake Tang Dynasty clay horse, they will be all over you like hair on a gorilla. The Chinese vendor immediately smells a sale. He or she quickly and silently slithers over to you to close in for the kill.

There are some simple rules to follow:

- Only stop at a stall or open-air shop where there are some tchotchkes of real interest.
- Do not look the vendors in the eyes but continue to stare at the item. Otherwise, like a snake charmer, they will start to weave their spell on you. They will tell you about the amazing qualities of the item, who made it, how many generations of artisans it took to perfect this craft, and why you should purchase at least two.
- If you are interested in a particular souvenir item, never accept the price they offer. Always try offering the vendor one-fifth to one-tenth of their price as your starting offer. Almost everything that's for sale in China has a price that's negotiable.

How to Bargain

You can haggle over the price for just about everything in China. It's a game that all Chinese play when they shop at a store or a vendor's stall. If you as a foreign tourist don't play the game, they think of you as a real chump. If you end up paying anything close to the original asking price, you've been had. It's as if every shop in China is like your local car dealer. Your average car salesman asks you to pay $16,000 for a Honda Civic, knowing that you will eventually haggle the price down to $14,000 and get him to throw in a free keyless remote and a free CD player.

But imagine if the car dealership had a sticker price of $80,000 for that Honda Civic, expecting you to be smart enough to know that it should really go for $14,000 with the keyless remote and

CD player added for good measure. Now imagine that just about every store in America was like a car dealership. The sticker price is only a starting point for a heated negotiation between the salesperson and the customer over the final price of the item. You then have a picture of what it's like to shop in China. There are some major exceptions where haggling is not allowed, such as in hotels, restaurants, supermarkets, department stores, bookstores, and pharmacies.

In most other places of business, however, from giant electronic stores to small shops and street stalls, bargaining over the price is fair game.

Here's how the game is played. You see a purse that you like. You innocently ask the price. If you were Chinese, the shopkeeper or vendor might ask for 80 yuan. Seeing your foreign face, however, which looks to them like a giant dollar sign with a mouth, they ask you for 200 yuan. A Chinese person would know from experience what a certain kind of item is probably worth and offer to pay a little less than that. You as a foreigner have no idea. 200 yuan is only approximately US$25, so it actually seems like a good deal. Wow, this may be a real bargain and you hand over the 200 yuan. Man, did you blow it! It's not just that you have paid two and a half times what the item should have sold for, you have actually encouraged the vendor to continue to jack up the price of things for foreigners.

The Chinese merchant will be all the more likely to eye greedily any tourist who walks by his shop in the same way a spider views a fly, or a cat views a mouse, or a political canvasser views an open door.

Here is the way the Chinese would purchase the purse. You should follow their example. Since most things in China are usually not one of a kind, but available from countless other shops or stalls in that same neighborhood—often a few feet away—never buy anything without comparative shopping. See what other vendors will ask for that same purse. The first vendor asked you for 200 yuan, but at another shop you see the same purse and they ask you for 100 yuan. In a third shop you overhear the shopkeeper offer the exact same purse to a Chinese tourist for 80 and the Chinese ends up paying only 50 yuan. Then you know what the going price should really be.

Below is a sample conversation between a Chinese shopkeeper and a savvy tourist:

Shopkeeper: You like that painting? It's by very famous local artist. Very beautiful.
Tourist: How much?
Shopkeeper (after a contemplative pause, for added effect):

I give it to you for 200 yuan.

Tourist: That's way too expensive. How about 50 yuan?

Shopkeeper: 50 yuan?! (Shaking his head and laughing) No, no, way too little. How about 150 yuan?

Tourist: That's way too much. Forget it! (starts to walk away)

Shopkeeper: OK, OK. To make a friend, only 50 yuan.

Tourist: 40.

Shopkeeper: OK, OK, only 40.

Enjoy the game. The shopkeepers and vendors will respect you more if you haggle with them. It's a way of life. Some foreigners don't like the hassle of always bargaining for every souvenir. It can get pretty tiring after a while. The truth is that pretty soon you will get used to the pricing system and bargaining actually becomes easier. Some of our students actually claim they miss it when they return home, where they're tempted to bargain down the price of Pop-Tarts with the cashier in the checkout lane of their local supermarket!

The Aggressive Vendor

Of all the obstacles the tourist faces on a Chinese city street, perhaps the most troublesome and the most annoying is the aggressive itinerant vendor. Not all people who are trying to sell you things in China have their own shop or market stall. Many are small-scale sellers with only a few choice souvenir items they want to foist on tourists. They congregate around the famous

tourist sites waiting for their chance to pounce. This is a true cat and mouse game, and you're the mouse!

Let's say you go to see the world famous tomb of the Qin (pronounced "chin") Emperor. You spend a few hours alongside hundreds of other tourists gawking at the nearly seven thousand terra-cotta soldiers that have guarded this tomb for more than two thousand years. It's time to head back to the hotel. You have that satisfied feeling that indeed your trip to China has been worth it. For you have seen what the Chinese claim is the eighth man-made wonder of the world and it was spectacular. You have gotten a glimpse of what the army of the first emperor of China looked like. You have stepped back in time.

Feeling at peace with the world, you exit the museum area and begin walking back to where you can board your waiting bus or taxi. What you haven't been prepared for is a living army of itinerant vendors from the countryside. Each is armed with a single small box that contains exactly the same thing—four small replicas of the terra-cotta warriors and their horses. You make the mistake of casually looking inside one of the boxes as you pass the first vendor. It is then that he begins his cry of "one dallah, one dallah" (English translation: "one dollar," i.e., "going cheap"). You hurry by the first vendor only to be accosted by a second . . . and a third and a fourth. You walk faster now, trying not to look at the other vendors. They hurry after you, thrusting their box in front of you to give you a close look at the bargain they're offering you. Shouting "no, no" or, if you know Chinese, "bú yào, bú yào" ("boo yow, boo yow" = not want, not want), you try to hurry by. Breaking into a slow trot you make it to within sight of the parking lot. You're home free now, you think. You breathe a sigh of relief.

Suddenly you see in front of you a group of vendors blocking your way, making a last ditch stand to prevent you from leaving the tourist site without buying something useless. The most aggressive of the pack follows alongside you for twenty or thirty paces. He grabs your arm, insisting that you cannot live without four small clay warriors in a box. You tell him you wouldn't want his box of bric-a-brac even if it were free. He presses you all the more closely until you tell him to shove off. He curses you in Chinese and finally heads off to harass another victim.

You have just witnessed one of the downsides of the new capitalism in China. For the first three decades of Communist rule little free enterprise was allowed. Now that almost anything can be sold freely in China, every peasant and his grandmother seems to be out on the street trying to make a fast buck. The Chinese slogan has changed from Mao's "Serve the people" to Deng Xiaoping's "Suck people dry." OK, the famous quote attributed to Deng is really "To get rich is glorious." But "suck people dry" is the phrase that's caught on, it appears. You begin to miss the days when all Chinese wore Mao jackets and the only things for sale on the street were Popsicles or watermelon. Now that there is an army of vendors on the march in China, trying to sell you anything they can get their hands on, how is the lone tourist to face such an assault?

Shopping in Large Stores

Say you decide to take refuge from the aggressive street vendors by shopping in a department store. Or you'd like to buy something from a large bookstore or pharmacy.

In these kinds of stores the salespeople are far less aggressive than the small shop owners or street vendors. That's because they're not the owners but only employees and often don't care that much whether you buy something or not. They're also behind counters, so they can't easily seize you by the arm. You figure you're safe now and it'll be just like shopping in a large store in America.

You'd be right except for one thing. The way you pay for things. In every larger store in China except for supermarkets the Chinese have made the process of paying for what you'd like to buy as complicated and as time-consuming as possible. Say you go to a department store. On the first floor you find a lovely pair of earrings in the shape of panda bears. You decide that they're a bargain at 80 yuan (around US$10). You hold out 80 yuan to the store clerk, but instead of giving you the earrings, she gives you a bill for the earrings and motions for you to go thirty feet away to a cashier's counter. It's there that you have to "wait in line" to pay for your earrings and get a receipt. You then take the receipt back to the clerk who will finally hand over the earrings. It seems that the store doesn't feel that you can trust one person to both handle the merchandise and handle money, too. No, those are separate jobs, each of which requires someone with specialized expertise. In our family, for instance, Qin is good at handling money while Larry is only good at taking things down off shelves. Hmm, maybe the Chinese have a point after all!

Anyway, just in making one purchase you get in some pretty good exercise running back and forth between the counter with the merchandise, the cashier's stand, and back to the counter again. If you find a pair of swim fins on the second floor, you'll have to go through the same thing all over again on the second floor that you went through on the first. Swim fins are a different section of the store and you must pay for each item at the cashier's stand in each separate department. If you buy one item on all six floors of the department store you will have run pretty much the equivalent of a marathon by the time you've completed all your purchases.

This system is aggravating enough if you're completely sound of limb. The time it became almost too much to bear was when Larry was hit by a bicyclist, in Shanghai, and his foot was broken. He also had numerous cuts and bruises on his knees and legs, which were bleeding profusely. He hobbled into a pharmacy nearby, where he was told he needed to go up to the second floor for disinfectant and bandages. Since the pharmacy was one of the older government-run businesses, there was no elevator or escalator. It took him five minutes of excruciating pain to hop on one foot up the long staircase to the second floor. It was comical and pathetic at the same time. He asked for disinfectant and bandages, along with some tape to hold the bandages. The clerks took the things off the shelves, but since this was China they couldn't give him the merchandise.

Instead they handed him the various charge slips for the three purchases and pointed to the cashier's desk. It was all the way across the floor from the counter where he was leaning. Dragging his broken foot behind him it took him what seemed another five minutes to hobble over to the cashier, pay for the items, and then return to where the supplies he needed were waiting for him. What made things worse was that the temperature that day was around 95 degrees, with a humidity of at least 101%. And, there was no air-conditioning on the second floor of the store, not a fan or even a single window.

To be fair, it was then that Larry was reminded of how very nice the Chinese can often be to foreigners. They're not always trying to rip us off. Several of the women clerks in the pharmacy finally took pity on the sweating, bleeding, hobbling middle-aged American. They put Larry in a room nearby, sat him down, turned on a fan, and set to disinfecting and bandaging his wounds themselves as if this were a hospital rather than a drugstore. These ladies not only soothed the physical wounds that Larry had suffered. They also helped heal the wounds to the spirit he had felt by the bicyclist who had not stopped when she knocked him over in the street.

Airports for Domestic Flights (Warning about Boarding!)

If you are flying into or out of China, there is little or no difference from international flights elsewhere. However, if you are taking a domestic flight within the country, you need to be prepared for the fact that Chinese airlines do not usually announce when they are preparing to board. If the occasional airline or airport should be so considerate as to make such announcements, you will notice long before that happens that the majority of Chinese passengers for that flight will already be crowding the entrance to the gate, ready to rush through when the announcement should come. The reason is that for the past half century, the lack of goods and services has accustomed the Chinese to rush forward, pushing and shoving if necessary, to make sure they get what they want. They have developed what seems to be a sixth sense, a survival instinct, that tells them when something is about to open up.

Therefore you can't just sit and relax near the gate, reading a book or magazine as most of us are accustomed to doing in the West before a flight, waiting for your seating section to be called to board. And do not expect that the Chinese passengers will go

through the gate in an orderly manner.

You need to be vigilant like a Thomson's gazelle that's grazing on the African plain. When the herd starts to run, the wise gazelle starts running, too. It doesn't look around to see whether lions are coming. It just takes off with the herd. So be a wise gazelle. Watch what others are doing. If the Chinese passengers start to line up by the gate, even if you hear no announcement whatsoever, follow them! Words to live by when taking a domestic flight in China are: First line up, then confirm. Otherwise, you will end up being one of the last passengers to get on the plane when the gate does suddenly open up for boarding, with no prior warning. If you have carry-on luggage, you are bound to discover that you may have no place to store your things.

On domestic flights within China, the baggage restrictions are much more severe. If you are flying economy class, you may be charged a hefty fee for any luggage exceeding 20 kilos (44 pounds), with a few airlines setting the limit at a mere 15 kilos; if you are flying business class, the limit is 30 kilos (66 pounds), and, in a blow to egalitarianism, first-class travelers are allowed a whopping 40 kilos (88 pounds) per person. If you're even five pounds over the allowed weight, you could end up paying as high a penalty as the whole ticket cost. Usually this is not the case, and fortunately, if you are traveling as a couple or a family, the airlines will average the weight of all your checked luggage. If the average weight of each passenger's bag is only 20 kilograms, you're fine. One trick is to put all your heaviest items in your backpack or some other carry-on item. You should be aware, however, that you're only allowed one carry-on item, not counting your camera or purse. And the carry-on can't exceed five kilos (a little over ten pounds).

Going through the security check at Chinese airports is pretty much the same as in airports in the U.S. In neither country are you allowed to take any liquids including water through the scanning area. However, after you've passed through security at an American airport, you can then fill your empty bottles with water from the drinking fountains or buy drinks at the airport kiosks to take on board with you. Not so in Chinese airports. Even when you are about to go through your gate, airline personnel will stop you from bringing any liquids on board. So our advice is to drink whatever water or other beverages you'd like while in the airport waiting area, but to not try to take any liquids with you when you board. You'll have to rely on the flight attendants to keep you hydrated while in the air.

In our experience at Chinese airports, we have observed two curious things about security checks. One is that we have never seen passengers be asked to take off their shoes. Seemingly the Shoe Bomber scare is not as acute as in the West. The other thing is that in spite of a lack of concern about footware there is a heightened sense of security at Chinese airports in the past few years. This has resulted not only in a greater number of security hurdles through which one must pass, but also has meant more and more pat-down searches of passengers. What's curious here is that while every man is patted down, by a woman no less, the women are usually just waved through! Whatever happened to equality between the sexes, which the Chinese government has ballyhooed for decades?!

China's new airports are remarkably efficient, but in a land of 1.3 billion, let's face it: there can be screw-ups. On a recent domestic flight within China, we got up at 5:00 A.M. in order to take a cab from our mountain village in Sichuan Province. For two hours we bounded along a winding road in the midst of mile-high mountains close to the Tibet border. Tired and carsick, we were relieved to reach the airport early, arriving at 8:00 A.M. to catch our 9:30 A.M. flight to the provincial capital of Chengdu.

We were holding tickets but needed to get boarding passes and it took us an excruciatingly long time to reach the ticket counter because several large tour groups had arrived just a moment before, jamming up all the available ticket agents. After waiting for at least thirty minutes, our turn finally came. We handed our tickets to the airline representative. We were then told that our Chinese travel agency, the largest in China, had apparently failed to confirm *one* of our tickets. It was Larry's. So we had one good ticket for the flight out. Since airlines routinely oversell their flights, this meant that all the available seats were taken by members of the large tour group in front of us. We panicked, but the airline representative shoved one ticket back to us with all the concern she would have shown had we told her the Chicago White Sox had failed to win the 1959 World Series.

When we insisted she do something for us, she finally agreed to put us on the next flight out. She handed us our boarding passes and, relieved, we started to go through security. We immediately turned back, however, when we realized that our bags had been checked through on the flight from which we had been dropped. We wanted our luggage to be on the same plane with us, since we had to pick them up for a connecting flight. So Qin had to go back behind the counter into the baggage security area to find our suitcases, bring them back out, and have them properly re-tagged for the new flight. Of course, this meant having the bags x-rayed again. This time, the security workers spotted something odd in Qin's bag. It turned out to be a can of hair spray.

We headed once again to the gate entrance, ready to sail through security. They wouldn't let Larry through, however. That was because the boarding pass the woman had given Larry didn't have his name, Lawrence Roy Herzberg, on it. No, the name on the boarding pass was Samuel Luk Wong. We already knew that Chinese travel agencies or airlines often misspell foreigners' names. In fact, there is a rule that says if fewer than three letters of your name are misspelled on your airline ticket and/or boarding pass, it's OK. It doesn't have to completely match the name on your passport. Qin had gone through China taking domestic flights where her name on her ticket always read Qing Herzber instead of Qin Herzberg. No problem. Only two letters in the name on her ticket differed from her passport. But Samuel Luk Wong was more than three letters different from Lawrence Roy Herzberg!

Larry had to go back and stand in line again so that he could get a boarding pass that actually had his name on it. No apology or explanation was given. When he was given his boarding pass, Larry had naively assumed that it would have his name on it. Always check your boarding pass to make sure all the information is correct.

There's another potential snafu of which you should be aware, one that on our last trip to China almost made us miss our flight back to the U.S. There are two Shanghai airports. Now that, in and of itself, should not be particularly surprising. After all, the Shanghai metropolitan area, with at least seventeen million people, is China's largest city. America's largest city, New York, has two airports, namely Kennedy and LaGuardia. There are two airports in both Paris and London. It only makes sense that Shanghai, which along with Beijing is the biggest hub for both international and domestic travel in China, should also have two airports. The only problem is that travel agents in the West are not always aware of which airport it is when they are making a booking; if they see "Shanghai" that's good enough for them, but it may put you in a bit of a pinch.

What we didn't notice until the previous day was that our flight from Xiamen to Shanghai was scheduled to arrive at the Shanghai Hongqiao Airport, where most domestic flights land, but that our flight back to the U.S. would leave from the newer

Shanghai Pudong Airport, which handles all international flights. The airports are separated by exactly 50 kilometers (about 30 miles). For us, that meant negotiating 30  miles of congested highway and clogged roads in China's biggest city. Our travel agent back home in the States had only allowed two hours from our arrival time until our international flight home was scheduled to depart, not realizing two different Shanghai airports were involved.

Fortunately, we were able to contact the local Chinese travel agent in Xiamen, who booked us on a much earlier flight to Shanghai, so we could make the connection easily. We got on the one-and-a-half-hour flight from Xiamen to Shanghai Hongqiao and arrived five hours before our flight took off from Shanghai Pudong Airport to the U.S. Everything seemed OK, but we should have known better. The Murphy of "Murphy's Law" would have loved it in China. Anything really can and really will go wrong. As is true with so many domestic flights within China, the plane will not always taxi to the gate. Instead it leaves you out on the tarmac, where you exit down a moveable stairway to a waiting shuttle bus to take you to the terminal. We crowded on to the shuttle, the doors closed, and we were waiting to make the two-minute ride to the gate when a big commotion suddenly arose.

A middle-aged man started yelling that he couldn't find the big bundle of money he had put in his bag in the overhead compartment of the plane. Someone on the plane had definitely stolen his money during the flight, he claimed. When he went to exit the aircraft, he discovered that his bag in the overhead compartment was partially open and the gloves which had been inside had fallen to the floor of the plane. Airline employees ran frantically back into the plane to search and in the meantime a police car drove up. Our shuttle bus was going nowhere as an investigation ensued.

A policeman got on the shuttle bus and started questioning the man and the people around him. As the minutes went by, one Chinese man started shouting that he would gladly waive his right against being searched so that he could be cleared and go on his way without further delay, and tried to convince others to do the same. Time dragged on, with the Chinese passengers on the shuttle growing more and more impatient. The four other foreigners on the bus besides Qin and Larry did not understand at all the drama that was being played out, and just stared uncomprehendingly at the shouting Chinese passengers.

When it was hinted that all the passengers might be searched and their carry-on items examined, the man who had lost his money started shouting that he had found his money on the floor of the shuttle bus. Obviously the police ruse had worked and the thief in his panic had dropped the envelope with the money that he had pilfered. In today's China, Communist state that it is, citizens cannot be searched arbitrarily by police—at least not so publicly as this would have been.

In any case we were free to go. Once again, however, we were reminded that travel in China can always throw unexpected obstacles in your path, even when everything seems to be going swimmingly.

If your flight in China is cancelled or seems to be delayed indefinitely, do not panic or try to exchange your tickets for another flight. Frankly, it's just too much of a hassle to retrieve your bags, stand in line to change your tickets, try to find a hotel near the airport for the night, and then contact the people who were supposed to pick you up and won't know that you didn't stick with your original flight.

Riding the Rails

China is building highways at a furious pace, and the Chinese are now buying more cars than Americans. At the same time, the country has vastly upgraded its railway system. Traveling by train offers many advantages over flying. You don't need to arrive at the train station nearly as early as you do when checking in at an airport. There is no luggage to check for train travel, and no series of security checks or pat-downs to be endured; you need only one cursory security check at the train station entrance. Much of a country can be seen from the windows of a train, whereas there is usually little to be seen from the air except clouds. You can get up and walk around in a train, and you can choose a great variety of food and drink from the carts that are wheeled past you in the aisles. Taking a train can thus be a superior choice to flying, as long as the trains are fast enough to compete with planes in getting you from one place to the next. Fortunately, China between many major cities now offers "bullet trains" that make riding the rails an attractive alternative to air travel.

Domestic trains are differentiated by classes based on speed and level of service. A letter (G, D, T, K, and Z) preceding the number indicates the type of train. The letters are derived from the first letter in transliterated English of the Chinese name for the train. "G" trains ("gāosù tiělù" / high-speed railroad) are the fastest, averaging speeds well over 300 kph (188 mph). They usually just serve two end-points, with some making a few intermediate stops. The "D" trains (dòngchē / fast-moving trains) are also high-speed trains and are the next fastest. They only run during the day for short distances between major cities, and are fairly few in number. Their top speed is generally 250 kph (155 mph). The "T" ("tè kuài" /express) and "K" ("kuàichē" / fast speed) trains, with top speeds of 140 kph (87 mph) and 120 kph (75 mph) respectively, are the slower, older trains, despite their names in Chinese. The "T" trains make fewer stops between cities; the "K" trains make frequent stops, usually on the half hour. Most trains in China are "K" trains. Finally the "Z" trains (zhídá/ direct express) are overnight express trains with sleeping compartments and are the best choice for catching some zzz's, as the name suggests to English speakers. Their top speed is 160 kph (100 mph).

"G" and "D" Trains

The trains of most interest to foreign travelers are the "G" and "D" trains. These are the Chinese "bullet trains" that can reach speeds up to 350 kph (218 mph). For energy conservation as well as safety reasons, these trains average only around 315 kph (197 mph). The trip from Beijing to Shanghai by "G" train covers over 1,300 kilometers (807 miles) in only four hours, including three stops in cities like Jinan and Nanjing, and costs only 933 yuan (US$150) for first class, which is cheaper than flying. The airports in Beijing and Shanghai have the worst record for on-time departures of any major airports in the world. Only 28% of flights out of Shanghai and a mere 18% out of Beijing leave within fifteen minutes of their scheduled departure time! The "G" trains, on the other hand, generally leave on schedule.

To be fair, however, that was not true for our first experience. Our train was scheduled to leave Beijing at 10:00 A.M. Fifteen minutes before departure we were comfortably seated with our considerable amount of luggage stowed at the back of the train car. Many moments later we noticed that although our watches read 10:10, we had still not left the station. Suddenly an announcement was made, only in Chinese, that the train wasn't functioning properly and that we needed to change trains. Fortunately we understand Chinese, but the other Americans only realized what was happening when they saw all the Chinese passengers hurriedly rise from their seats almost in unison and, grabbing their bags, make a mad dash for the exits. A bit out of breath but seated once again in our new train, we finally took off at 10:25. An apology was made to the passengers in English as well as in Chinese. All announcements on "G" trains are made in both languages, after all. They had simply neglected the English translation for the unexpected change of trains! Most likely this will not happen to you, but we have taken the bullet trains in Japan nearly a hundred times and this has never befallen us before. But it did happen on our very first bullet train ride in

China. We could only turn to each other and exclaim "TIC!" ("This is China!").

Nevertheless, we highly recommend taking the "G" train at least once while traveling around China. In addition to the Beijing–Shanghai route, these ultra-fast trains run between Beijing and Guangzhou, 2,298 kilometers (1,427 miles) in eight hours, with stops in Shijiazhuang, Zhengzhou, Wuhan, and Changsha. Second-class tickets are 865 yuan (US$141), one-way; first-class tickets are 1,383 yuan ($225), almost exactly the cost of a one-way plane ticket, economy class, for the three-hour flight; business class is 2,727 yuan ($445). There are also "G" trains between Beijing and Tianjin, Shanghai and Nanjing, Shanghai and Hangzhou, Nanjing and Ningbo via Hangzhou, Guangzhou and Wuhan, Zhengzhou and Xian, and Harbin and Dalian. Very soon all the major cities in China will be connected by high speed rail. The "G" trains operate independently of other trains in China. The facilities at "G" train stations are first-rate and on a par with those at modern airports.

For all the many good things about the high-speed and comfortable "G" trains, there are some things of which the traveler should take note. The overhead compartments are only wide enough to accommodate small suitcases of the airplane "carry-on" variety or slightly larger. Big American-size suitcases need to be stored in a luggage rack at the back of each car. There is only room for six big suitcases there, so the rest have to be placed on the ground in front of the luggage rack. Fortunately, the Chinese travelers never have suitcases so large that they need to use this rack. So as long as there are not many Western travelers in your train car, you'll have no problem. Do try to enter the car at the rear, however, so that you can first stow your big suitcases in the rack before finding your reserved seat.

Be aware that the seat numbers are a bit deceptive. Seats A and C are next to each other, as are D and F. So remember—not ABCD, but ACDF!

"G" trains begin boarding approximately thirty minutes before departure time and will not allow anyone to board less than ten minutes prior to departure. After finding out from which number "gate" (检票口/"check-ticket-gate") your train will board, line up to show your ticket to the attendant when the turnstiles open the half hour or so before the train is scheduled to leave. Chinese citizens have to show their national I.D. card. For foreign visitors it's enough to just flash your passport, which the attendant will not bother to check.

Once you're underway you can expect an enjoyable journey. The cars in "first class" are nicely air-conditioned. The fairly cushy seats recline at least 30 degrees. There's even a place to plug in your laptop and recharge it. "First class," comfortable as it is, is actually not the highest class of seating. There is a "business class" car with even nicer amenities. But "first class" is certainly pleasant enough. Attendants will periodically come through the aisles with carts loaded with various snack foods and drinks for purchase. The only complimentary service provided is a small snack box that contains sugared green peas in a tiny package labeled U.S.A.; a tiny brick of jellied crabapple candy; a pellet of hard candy called Alpenliebe with a strawberry and crème flavor, made by an Italian company; and a small square of vanilla wafer. You're also given a peach drink juice box.

Makes airline food seem a gourmet delight! But to be fair, you'll get no better snack on flights between Beijing and Shanghai.

Be sure to look over the train's on-board magazine provided in the seat pocket in front of you. It contains some of the most delightful English you'll encounter in China, including the poetic description of the trip you're about to enjoy: "Sitting with thousand miles of beauty." The "travel notice" contains much important advice, such as: "When getting on and off the train, please queue up and let passengers get off first. Don't push. . . . Crawling under the train or climbing up the train is not allowed. Please do not jump off the platform or get into the orbit. . . . There is an emergency escape window, with a red spot on it, and a hammer in four corners of each carriage. In time of emergency, hold the breaking window emergency hammer tightly and hit the window on the right spot. Then push the incompletely broken glasses outwards with the handle frame. The action is only allowed in time of emergency. . . . If an emergency happens during the trip, the passengers shall not panic. If a fire accident happens, use water or extinguisher to put out the fire. However, if a fire hazard or explosion happens, the train must be stopped immediately. The staff will immediately start up the evacuation when the train is stabilized. Please do not jump off the train while the train is still in motion, so as to avoid any unnecessary hurt or death."

We would like to express our sincere wish that none of you will experience any unnecessary hurt or death, while traveling by train or at any other time!

What is even more delightful about the "G" trains is that clean Western sit-down toilets are provided, similar to those on airplanes. Next to the toilet compartments is a large area with a sink that includes motion-controlled water faucets and soap dispensers, and even a hand-dryer. These are luxuries not taken for granted by those familiar with the average Chinese public restroom!

For an even more wonderful "G" train experience, try to book seats in the "sightseeing area" at the front of the train. This small seating area is right behind the driver's cabin and holds only four seats in what amounts to a business-class compartment. There is as much leg room as in first class on an airplane, but with much more of a sense of privacy.

"D" Train Travel Tips

The "D" trains, such as the ones that run between Shanghai and Suzhou and between Shanghai and Hangzhou, are also a good choice for the foreign traveler. Air-conditioned and with comfortable seating, and traveling at an average of 240 kph (150 mph), the one-hour ride from Shanghai to Suzhou or the one-and-a-half-hour trip to Hangzhou is most enjoyable. A first-class ticket from Shanghai to Hangzhou is 123.50 yuan, only a little over US$20. This is definitely the fastest, cheapest, and most sensible way to now travel between these popular destinations.

For "D" trains there is nobody to take your ticket at the gate. When boarding begins, simply put your ticket into an automatic machine, being sure to retrieve it after you go through the turnstile. You'll need to show it on leaving the station at your destination. "D" trains only begin boarding fifteen minutes prior to departure and stop boarding three minutes prior, a shorter amount of time than the "G" trains allow. So do check your ticket right away to find which car you'll be in. Then look for the car numbers painted on the ground of the train platform after you're allowed to pass through the gate and await the train there. Now when the train comes you'll be somewhere close to where you need to get on and not have to drag your luggage in a panic across the entire platform to get to your car. Those of you who are veterans of train travel in Europe and/or Japan are used to this. Given the sorry state of our passenger rail system in the U.S., however, most Americans are unused to train travel, so we thought it best to review the basics, just to make sure no one gets left behind.

"T" and "K" Trains

The slower and older "T" and "K" trains only average around 120 kph, a little over 70 mph. Because of their slower speed, their lack of storage space for big suitcases, and their inferior facilities, we would advise that they only be taken by foreign tourists who are energetic and adventurous, who have little luggage beyond a large backpack, and who want to rub elbows with ordinary Chinese people. It would be best if these Western travelers can also speak a little Chinese.

The "K" trains are popular with the average Chinese person because they're really cheap. And they stop in many smaller cities that are not serviced by the much faster and more expensive "G" and "D" trains. For instance, a "K" train from Nanjing to Yangzhou, a distance of 43 miles, only costs 27.50 yuan, or around US$4.50. And a "K" train from Shanghai to Yangzhou, a distance of 390 miles, costs but 97.50 yuan, which is only a little more than $16. And that's for a first-class "soft seat" ticket in an air-conditioned car!

There are many different classes of seats on the "T" and "K" trains. For shorter distances there are cars with soft, cushioned seats, known as "soft seat," as well as cars with wooden seating, known as "hard seat." A ticket in a soft seat car is obviously more expensive than one in a hard seat car. The soft seat and hard

seat cars are further divided into those with air conditioning and those without. You naturally pay a bit more to be in an air-conditioned car. Even though going without air conditioning only saves 10 or 20 yuan, many Chinese opt to go without.

At the Shanghai train station for the "T" and "K" trains you will see porters wearing red T-shirts and red vests with yellow characters on them approach passengers in the waiting area with a lot of luggage and offer to help with their suitcases. If you are traveling with a lot of bags, you might want to pay them the 10 yuan (US$1.65) for a large suitcase and 6 yuan ($1.00) for a small one to have them take your bags for you to the platform. This will also entitle you to descend to the platform some minutes ahead of the other passengers, who otherwise have to wait in line for the gates to open to go down the escalator or stairs to the waiting train. You don't pay the porter directly, by the way. He will take you around the barrier to a clerk on the edge of the waiting area, who will take your money. You then follow the porter to the platform.

There are many reasons why the average Western tourist will want to avoid the "K" train. They travel at slow speeds and make frequent stops. There is a far greater chance of a delay than there is with the "G" and "D" trains, sometimes as much as an hour. They only offer squat toilets that quickly become very dirty and unpleasant. These metal squat toilets are particularly small, because the room itself is so tiny. If you want to take proper aim at the hole, your head and body need to touch the wall. But that is to be avoided at all costs. So the unsavory choice for the average-size American is to either dirty your clothes by leaning against the wall or making a mess on the floor.

On the "K" trains there is no place to stow luggage bigger than small suitcases that can be hoisted into the overhead shelving. We were allowed to keep our huge suitcases in the area between cars but were told by the train employees that we needed to get up at every stop to make sure no one had left the train with our bags.

For your entertainment pleasure, easy listening music will be played periodically over the loud speakers. This is great, if you're not trying to sleep or read, and if your taste runs to Chinese soft rock ballads. The music will be interrupted, however, by a long discourse in Chinese on the different benefits of every kind of fruit. If you understand the language, you will appreciate the invaluable advice that eating more than four oranges a day may cause your body to overheat. You'll be interested to know that cherries are recommended as an ideal fruit for travelers. You'll also be informed as to which plants are edible and which are poisonous, and what to do if you are poisoned by eating the wrong plants. No English ever comes over the loudspeakers on "T" or "K" trains. If we still haven't convinced you that "K" trains may not be for you, let us add that on "K" trains you very likely will be treated to a sales pitch from a train employee, who will be hawking shoe inserts and nylon socks that don't run or tear. Unbelievably, nearly half the people in our car bought the shoe inserts, which sold for only 25 yuan!

Even on the "K" trains, though, carts loaded with food and drink for sale will be periodically pushed down the aisles. There is often a great variety of fresh fruit. Beer, too, is available. A cheap box lunch with a meat cutlet and rice may be among the offerings. The cart pushers are usually pretty young women wearing a blue uniform with a bold red tie. Let it not be said that the "K" trains show no sense of fashion!

In a country with around a third of the world's smokers (over 50% of Chinese men are heavy smokers), the good news is that all trains in China, including the "K" trains, are by rule smoke-free. By and large you can count on no one smoking in any train car in the country when the train is moving. However, especially on the "K" trains, some Chinese men do try to smoke by the exit doors when the train is stopped at a station. You will likely smell smoke wafting into your car at those times.

Sleeping Cars

The long distance "K" trains, as well as the express "Z" trains, offer sleeping cars. There are three types of accommodation: Hard Class, Soft Class, and Deluxe Soft Class. Most Chinese choose the Hard Class sleeping cars. The cars contain many compartments. Each compartment usually has six bunks, with three on a side, although some will only have four bunks with two on a side.

There is only about two or three feet of vertical space between the middle bunk and the upper bunk, and between the upper bunk and the ceiling, so the arrangement is not for the claustrophobic. Submarine crew members should feel right at home! Our recommendation is to reserve a bottom bunk, where you have a reasonable amount of head room and where you can put your large American suitcases alongside you. If you've reserved one of the higher bunks, the train staff will insist that you put your bags up in a small area above the door frame inside the compartment, about eight feet above the ground and higher than the highest bunk bed. Even if you have the superhuman strength to lift your suitcase that high, there is simply not enough room up there for any large bags.

If you're not lucky enough to get a bottom bunk, hoist yourself up to one of the upper beds using the single small metal footstand that folds out from the wall just inside the compartment. These footstands are sufficient for young southern Chinese women and men who are small and agile to place their dainty feet and quickly scamper up to the higher bunks. But they are not made for the more gargantuan Western foot. The compartments in the Hard Sleeper cars are unenclosed and open to the narrow aisle, allowing you to eavesdrop on any conversations taking place there between people sitting in fold-down seats as they wait to clamber into their upper bunks for the night. The dining car on the train is not available to Hard Class passengers, so you'll also hear your fellow passengers snacking on the various provisions they've brought with them or purchased from the passing food carts. Traveling by Hard Class sleeper is a fairly fun experience for the foreigner who speaks some Chinese. There are some interesting conversations to be had with fellow passengers in this setting. But it's not recommended for the average Western tourist.

These "K" trains, which go everywhere and are so very cheap, are mainly used by the huge Chinese working class. More than two hundred million Chinese ride them from the countryside or smaller towns into the large cities for employment. And when country folk in China travel, they sometimes take their produce with them. So you will see them bring onto the train large boxes of fruit, vegetables, and even livestock. On a "K" train we took from Beijing to Datong in northern China we saw a notice that read "No more than 20 baby chicks per passenger may be taken aboard"!

If you do take a "K" train, the Soft Class sleeper is where you will want to be, providing you are in no great hurry to reach your destination and want to have a long-distance train adventure. In the Soft Class cars each compartment has four beds, with a lower and an upper one on each side. There is a large window with a small table under it. Within the room and extending over the outer aisle is usually a place to stow your luggage. Additional space is under the two lower bunks, which everyone in the car can share. On some trains, there is no overhead storage space and the space under the beds is limited by a steel bed frame. In that case you have to sit on your bed next to your luggage. The lower berths are more expensive than the upper ones, but are worth the additional cost. To spend many hours in a windowless upper bunk does not make for the most enjoyable train ride.

You will have quite a variety of compartment mates, which can be interesting and fun. Soft Class tickets are much more expensive than those in Hard Class, so you tend to get a different class of people. Some may be other foreigners or Chinese who speak some English.

Here is a sampling of the prices for Soft Class sleepers:

Shanghai to Beijing	478 yuan (US$77)
Beijing to Xian	400 yuan (US$65)
Guangzhou to Guilin	313 yuan (US$50)
Guilin to Xian	613 yuan (US$99)
Xian to Suzhou	466 yuan (US$75)
Hong Kong to Shanghai	Hong Kong $1,039 (US$134)

Deluxe Soft sleepers are compartments with only two beds. This is perfect for a couple, since you get a level of privacy missing from the other choices. Deluxe Soft sleepers tend to be more modern. You may have a closet in which you can hang things, and even an in-room sink and toilet. Many "Z" trains offer this kind of accommodation, but few "K" and "T" trains do.

If you're traveling long distances and want to save on a hotel room or allow more time for daylight sightseeing, your best option is the "Z" trains. These overnight express trains have few or no midway stops and are clearly superior to the "K" and "T" trains. "Z" trains operate between Beijing and Xian, Shanghai and Xian, and Beijing and Harbin.

As at the airports in China, beware of "black" cabs at train stations. You will likely be approached by several people offering you "Taxi . . . taxi"! They will motion to you to follow them or will attempt to take your luggage from you. These people are working for the "black" cabs, i.e., fake taxis, who want to "take you for a ride" at double or triple the price of a real taxi. Pay no attention to these people and do not make any eye contact with them. If they persist, just say "bu-yow" ("NO!") and move on. NEVER let someone else help you with your luggage. It could be the last time you ever see it! No railway employees or police officers will ever approach you, nor will legitimate taxi drivers.

When leaving a train station, if you are going to take a cab to your hotel rather than use the subway system connected to the station in the larger cities, head immediately for the taxi queue just outside the station. It will be to one side or the other beyond the exit.

Train Adventures

There are three exceptional train adventures to be had in China.

One is the first commercially operated high-speed magnetic levitation in the world, and one of only three worldwide—the Shanghai Maglev train. In less than eight minutes it covers a

distance of 30 kilometers (18 miles) to take passengers from the Shanghai International Airport in Pudong to the outskirts of central Pudong. From there you can then take the subway to the center of Shanghai.

The Maglev's maximum normal operation speed is 431 kph (268 mph), faster than any Formula One race car. This is not the most practical alternative for tourists flying into the Pudong Airport with a lot of luggage. But for those traveling light, it can be both a practical and thrilling way to begin your journey into Shanghai. The Maglev operates from 6:45 A.M. to 9:30 P.M., leaving every fifteen to twenty minutes. A one-way ticket costs 50 yuan (US$7.27), or 40 yuan ($5.81) for those passengers showing proof of an airline ticket purchase. If you're staying in Shanghai for a long enough period of time, you might even consider it a slightly expensive carnival ride, just to experience what it's like to float on a cushion of air at high speed.

A second very special train adventure is a trip to the old Silk Road in northwestern China. The Silk Road was the trade route that two thousand years ago connected the ancient Chinese capital of Chang-an, now Xian, with Rome. The best way to see the extraordinary landscape in this part of the country, as well as to visit the famous Dunhuang Caves, is by train (trains heading here are convenient, inexpensive, and offer both Soft and Hard sleepers). You will have to take your own toilet paper, soap or wet towels, and other toiletries. The best route is Xian—Jiayuguan Pass—Urumqi—Turpan—Kashgar—Hetian (desert crossing)—Aksu—Dunhuang.

The third special train adventure in China is the passenger rail to Tibet. Trains leave for the Tibetan capital of Llasa from Beijing, Chengdu, Chongqing, Shanghai, Guangzhou, Xining (in Tibet's neighboring Qinghai Province), and Lanzhou (in northwest China). These lines all travel through the Tanggula Pass, which at 16,640 feet above sea level is the world's highest railway. The journey includes the chance to see some of the world's most stunning mountain landscapes from the windows of a train. You'll definitely be "sitting with thousand miles of beauty" on this particular ride! Be aware that all tourists entering Tibet will need to obtain a Tibet Travel Permit.

If you would like to travel by train anywhere in China, ask a travel agency like CITS to buy your tickets for you well ahead of time. They will deliver your tickets to your hotel just prior to your trip. You can, of course, purchase tickets yourself at the train stations. But you will likely have to wait in a long line and may discover there are no tickets available for the train you wish to take. You will need to show your passport when buying tickets.

Do not attempt to buy train tickets online. The websites in English that claim to offer this service simply do not work. You can click all you want on your intended purchase but it will be to no avail!

Medical Emergencies

Given the various dangers that China presents, from kamikaze bikers and taxi drivers to food to which Western stomachs are not accustomed and viruses to which Westerners have never been exposed, you may find yourself needing some medical care during your time in the Middle Kingdom. Do not despair. Help for anything that ails you is definitely available.

If it's a mere cold or cough that you develop, you will find drugstores on many a major street. In the largest cities like Beijing and Shanghai you can find a Western pharmacy with everything from aspirin to Tylenol and Advil. In smaller cities, however, the pharmacies will carry Chinese brands of these same medicines, with lovely Chinese characters decorating the entire box or package. If you don't speak or read Chinese, not to worry. Simply act out your symptoms, such as sneezing or coughing all over the drugstore clerk. They'll soon get the idea as to what is troubling you, and rush to grab the appropriate antidote. Should they rush to the back room and not return after a half hour, you can safely assume they have been thoroughly grossed out by your overly effusive impression of a tubercular patient, and have retired for safety to the inner sanctum of the store. But if you don't overdo your demonstration, most likely they will hand over the preferred medication for your ailment.

Be aware, however, that in China there are two very different systems of medical treatments that are provided. One is the "modern," or "Western" one with which foreigners are familiar. The other system is that of traditional Chinese medicine, which uses acupuncture, moxibustion, and time-honored herbal remedies, instead of Western medicines, to treat various conditions. Each hospital has a wing devoted to Western medicine and another to traditional Chinese treatments. The same is true of the largest pharmacies. But in most cities in China pharmacies devote themselves to either one or the other system of treatment. If you simply ask someone to direct you to a nearby pharmacy or you see a store that looks like it might carry medicines with clerks in white uniforms, you may find yourself in a shop with drawer after drawer of herbs, berries, and deer antlers. So be sure to ask not just for a "yàofáng" ("yow-fahng") or "pharmacy," but a "xī yàofáng" ("see yowfahng") or "Western-style pharmacy" if it's aspirin or Tylenol you're looking for.

Be sure to bring a small first-aid kit to China. You may suffer minor cuts, which you can clean up on the go. Also bring your favorite cold medicine. Especially in the colder months, this can be essential. Upper respiratory ailments are extremely common in China, due to the crowding that brings people in close contact with others, as well as low standards of hygiene. Fall through spring is when you are most likely to get a cold or bronchitis, so be prepared by packing your preferred cold and cough remedies.

If you develop a really serious condition, such as having a heart attack upon seeing your hotel bill which includes all those little bottles of alcohol that you thought were complimentary but which were priced at 300 yuan per bottle, then the good folks at the front desk of the hotel will arrange for an ambulance to come and whisk you away to the nearest hospital that handles foreign guests.

The SOS International Alarm Center

If you have a medical problem that requires immediate attention, an even more trustworthy alternative is to call the SOS International twenty-four-hour "Alarm Center." In Beijing the number is (86)(10)6462-9100 (just dial the last eight digits if you're in Beijing); in Shanghai it is (86)(21)5298-9538 (just dial the last eight digits if you're in Shanghai). They will give you excellent advice and referrals to the best local facilities for foreigners. SOS International has its own clinics in four cities in China, including Beijing, Nanjing, Tianjin, and Shenzhen. These clinics mostly serve the expat community, as well as foreign tourists in need of immediate medical assistance. At costs similar to those in the U.S., which is extremely pricey by Chinese standards, they offer excellent facilities and medical expertise on a par with the best in the U.S., Canada, or England. Their highly qualified multinational staff of doctors, nurses, and lab technicians provide a wide range of health care services, diagnostic lab work, fully stocked pharmacies, and 24/7 emergency medical care.

On a recent trip to China, we spent four days in the beautiful

countryside of Wuyuan County in Jiangxi Province, visiting villages that are many centuries old. During our stay we were careful to drink only bottled mineral water, using it even to brush our teeth. We ate no meat, only vegetables and noodles. Since there were no restaurants in any of the ancient villages, including the one in which we were staying, we did have dinner at the home of a farm family that uses part of their home as a small inn. The green vegetables and eggplant the farmer's wife stir-fried for us were delicious, as was the melon soup she made. That was in large part because the vegetables had just been harvested that day from the farmer's own fields. The next day, Qin experienced intestinal discomfort that became more and more serious as the days went on. During the next three days she ate very little, since eating anything only made her diarrhea worse. Imodium did little or nothing to alleviate the problem. When we left the villages to spend a few days in the beautiful Lushan Mountains, Qin became more and more dehydrated as well as weaker and weaker from eating very little.

When she began to experience stomach cramps and became almost too weak to get up from bed, the hotel staff called us a cab to take us down the mountain to the nearest city, which was Jiujiang. They also contacted the CITS (China International

Travel Service) office in that city, since that organization had arranged our trip. A local guide and driver met us at a prearranged hotel, and after I quickly checked us in they hustled Qin off to what they claimed was the best hospital in town. Jiujiang is a city of 1.5 million people, but the emergency room looked like something from 1900 in a small city in the U.S. After registering, Qin was led to a dark and dingy room with a cement floor and eight beds, seven of which were already occupied by Chinese patients, with their relatives crowded around and with no curtains to separate one bed from another. The nurse tried to get Qin to lie down, but noticing that the sheets were stained and had obviously not been changed in some time, Qin declined. She was so weak that she could only walk with me supporting her on one side and the guide on the other. She desperately needed an IV, but refused to let them put one in. She had read horror stories of patients in Henan Province contracting HIV from an IV inserted with an unclean needle.

The young doctor in the emergency room did prescribe an antibiotic, as well as several other medicines to settle her stomach and to restore some salt into her system. While these treatments did allow her to feel well enough to fly to Beijing several days later, she was far from cured.

We were scheduled to fly back to the States in less than forty-eight hours and were concerned that she was in no condition to endure a twelve-hour flight while still suffering from diarrhea. It was then that Larry called the SOS twenty-four-hour "Alarm Center." It was 1:00 in the morning, but the friendly woman who immediately answered the phone and who could speak English well quickly transferred him to their SOS clinic. Within a few minutes Larry had made an appointment for

Qin to see a doctor from the Netherlands the very next morning.

We were very impressed by how clean, comfortable, and efficient the clinic was.

The doctor spoke excellent English and was caring and kind. After ordering a blood test be done on the premises and seeing the results, he prescribed a Western antibiotic, which he claimed would be much more effective than the Chinese antibiotic Qin had been given. We were able to fill the prescription quickly downstairs in their small but well-stocked pharmacy. A little more than twenty-four hours later, when we boarded the plane to the U.S., Qin was feeling well enough to make the trip without any real problem.

So we recommend the SOS clinics very highly. They even have a very nice coffee machine that dispenses complimentary cups of cappuccino, mocha, latte, and more! Expect to pay a whole lot for such excellent medical care, however. The total bill for the consultation with the doctor, the lab tests, and the prescriptions was over US$400! We still felt it was money well spent, given the circumstances.

Other Medical Options: Hotels vs. Hospitals

If, however, the medical problem you develop is neither rather minor nor extremely serious, but is somewhere in the gray area between a head cold and a heart attack, then there are certain things of which you should be aware.

First of all, pretty much any large hotel in China has a small medical staff on hand to help you with problems that can be treated on an outpatient basis. If you need a wound bandaged or an ingrown toenail attended to, refer to the hotel guide in your room or call the front desk and ask the location of the small clinic in the hotel.

The average hotel in China, however, lacks such a clinic. But the larger cities of China do have at least one hospital that is their very best and that has a special section devoted to treating foreign guests. Often these are referred to as "Number 1" hospitals. Western guests are not used to waiting in long lines all day at the hospital before they get to finally see a doctor. The Chinese, being aware of this and wanting to keep the tourist dollars flowing by providing speedier service for foreigners, have a small part of some of their hospitals ready to serve us, who will pay what to the Chinese are devilishly high prices for special medical care given by doctors who speak English.

Larry and Qin did not realize the above fact, however, and when Larry had his foot broken in Shanghai, the hotel clinic did not have an x-ray machine, nor could they give Larry a cast for his foot. They did, however, give us the name and address of the hotel that serves foreigners, and off we went in a cab to that location.

The taxi took us to the front entrance of the hospital, where we got out only to encounter a swarm of Chinese people outside the front door waiting to get in to see a doctor. Despairing of ever seeing a doctor that day or even that week, some thoughtful Chinese person pointed out to us that the entrance for foreigners was by another door. All we had to do was walk a block down the street, turn and walk another block, and we would find that special back entrance. The only problem was that Larry's foot was broken and he had no crutches. So here was this image of a pathetic, lame, middle-aged man with what appeared to be a clubfoot, dragging his aching body several blocks to the door by which foreigners are allowed to enter the hospital.

Once inside there was only a short wait before Larry was seen by a most competent doctor who, it was said, spoke some limited English but with whom we opted to speak his native language of Chinese. The good doctor told Larry that his foot needed to be x-rayed before he treated it. In came a thin man in his fifties pushing a wheelchair, who then proceeded to push Larry the two or three miles (or so it seemed) to the x-ray room in the Chinese part of the hospital. Larry's wheelchair was pushed past hundreds of Chinese people of all ages waiting in the hallway, then pushed ahead of all the Chinese waiting for x-rays, to come to a stop before a large x-ray machine that looked like it had been the top of the line—in the 1930s! But he didn't need to wait for hours for his x-ray, like all those Chinese people who had made their way to the hospital at the crack of dawn. Larry was treated like an honored foreign guest.

The x-ray machine confirmed that Larry indeed had a broken foot. The Chinese technician, on seeing Larry's foot, couldn't help from exclaiming: "What a big foot!" which, of course, made Larry feel so much better. It was another exhilarating ride in the wheelchair past hundreds of pairs of curious eyes as he was escorted back to the waiting doctor. The Chinese physician, with the help of a nurse, began to make a plaster cast in which to mummify Larry's foot. Only when Larry returned home to a specialist in Michigan did he discover that an American doctor would have instead given him a lightweight boot to wear on his foot, one that could be removed every evening so he could bathe. Instead Larry's foot looked like an appendage of King Tut, except that the bandages were whiter. And for only $10 or so he got a lovely pair of crutches to allow him to walk around and show off his new cast to the entire population of Shanghai. In this kind of upscale hospital with a specialty section for foreigners, you may pay by either credit card or cash. Upon returning home you can then send the receipt to your insurance company and be reimbursed for whatever is covered by your policy.

The upshot of this story is that you should make sure you find out whether the hospital to which you go for treatment has a special section for foreigners, and then have your taxi driver drop you in front of that entrance.

There is another important piece of information that you need to know regarding medical emergencies. You may have to go to a hospital in China to simply get some medical device or piece of equipment that is not available in a pharmacy. Crutches,

for instance. Or an oxygen tank! Take the case of Qin when she was with Larry in the town of Lijiang, set picturesquely in the mountains of the southwestern province of Yunnan, near Tibet. The altitude of the town is around 2,800 meters or roughly 8,400 feet. Unfortunately, it turned out that Qin's body could not adapt to the high altitude. The Chinese refer to people who can't swim or who don't like water as "hàn yāzi" or "dry-land duck." It seems that Qin was a "dīdì yāzi," or "low-land duck."

After a day walking around the mountains at nosebleed height, Qin was really having trouble breathing and was in need of supplementary oxygen.

Larry commandeered a taxi to take him to the nearest hospital to get some kind of oxygen tank. Fortunately, the driver, who was a chronologically gifted and kind man, had already guessed that Larry was unfamiliar with the procedure for obtaining an oxygen tank in a regular Chinese hospital, and actually went into the hospital with Larry to help. He first asked the way to the place where he could get Larry a portable supply of oxygen, asked the name of the piece of equipment, then went to a different part of the hospital where Larry had to pay first, then took the receipt from him back to the original place to obtain the oxygen. What they gave him, by the way, was a large flat pillow that seemed to be of no use in this emergency. But the hospital staff then proceeded to fill the pillow with oxygen and showed Larry that there was a tube attached to the pillow, which could then be attached to the patient's nose. It was through this that Qin could inhale the extra dose of oxygen she needed back in the hotel room. If you are not so fortunate as to have a compassionate cab driver to help you, make sure you are aware of the system in Chinese hospitals: "Pay first, get your respirator later."

In case you should have the misfortune to need medical attention someplace in China outside of the major cities, then you should be aware of the following: The only way to see a doctor or to get a prescription in China is to go to a hospital.

Doctors do not have separate offices as they do here in the U.S. Chinese hospitals are classified into four different levels in a hierarchy of quality and scope of medical care. So-called "international" hospitals like the Beijing Hospital are few in number and can only be found in Beijing. These are the top of the line. They are open to the general Chinese public, but the finest physicians and facilities are reserved for a section of the hospital open only to high Party officials and, of course, to foreigners.

The second tier of hospitals is that of the "city hospital." These offer care on a level that would be acceptable to foreigners. Such hospitals treat ordinary Chinese for surgeries and x-rays, and are well-run with decent equipment. This is the place for foreigners to go if they're not in Beijing, and it was to such a hospital Larry hobbled on his broken foot.

The third grade of hospital is the "district hospital." This is where Chinese go for treatment of common ailments like a cold, the flu, stomach troubles, cuts, and the like.

No surgical operations are performed here, but they feature both Chinese and Western medicines and also offer massage therapy and acupuncture treatment. This is definitely the cheapest place to go for a good massage, not only in China, but in most of the world.

The fourth and lowest level of medical care is provided by the small neighborhood or rural clinic. These are often just a few rooms in a shabby one-story building. It's sufficient for first aid and basic medical advice, and also allows Chinese in the neighborhood to renew and fill their prescriptions without having to make the trek to a large hospital.

A Visit to the Hospital

If you are a foreigner and develop a medical problem, then it's best to have your problem in Beijing. Otherwise go to a "city hospital," called "shìjí yīyuàn" ("shure-jee-ee-yuen"). Often the specific hospital of this type will have the words "rénmín" or "people's" hospital in the title. When you visit a regular hospital in China that does not have a section specifically reserved for foreigners, you will feel like you're in that interminable line of Chinese people as you wade through what seems to be the entire population of China just to get into the front door of the hospital.

For some, the size of the crowds can be intimidating beyond words. If you find yourself in a facility where you can only receive the same kind of treatment that the ordinary Chinese person receives when needing medical care, don't give up completely. It may seem ridiculously complicated, frustratingly slow, and full of humiliation, but it will only cost you time. Given the choice between seeing someone—anyone, and going it alone, we would argue that waiting for medical care is better than not waiting for it.

When you visit a Chinese hospital the first thing you do is to register or "guàhào" ("gwah-how") in the lobby, right inside the front door. The front door opens at 7:30 A.M., by which time the crowd of people who have been waiting outside since 5:00 or 5:30 that morning have already formed a long line ahead of you.

When you finally get into the lobby you will see several windows on each side.

If you're not sure which window is for registration, simply get in the longest line, because that's definitely the line for registration. When you finally make your way to the front of the line, you will pay a small amount of money to register, ten or twenty yuan, for which you receive a tiny, flimsy slip of paper with a number on it. Guard that little piece of paper as you would the most precious thing in the world, as this paper is the only proof you have that you registered for that day. You will need to figure out for yourself which department you need to register for, depending on your condition, from general internal medicine to osteopathy to gynecology to surgery.

Now you have to find out where in the hospital that department for which you registered might be hidden. When you find the right department you will usually see a desk in the front room, behind which sits a very stern-looking young

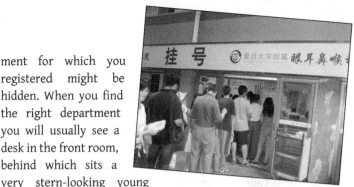

or middle-aged woman in a white uniform. Do not wrongly assume that this person, who works in a hospital, knows anything about medicine or has any sense of concern for the welfare of sick people. You duly hand over your flimsy slip of paper with your number on it to that lady. If you have been a patient in that hospital before, you also offer up your little booklet with your medical history, called a "bìnglì" ("bing-lee"). If this is your first visit to the hospital, you'll need to purchase a little blank booklet when you register.

Then you wait. Often there's no seat. Usually a hundred people are waiting there, sneezing, coughing, moaning, lying on benches or crouched on the floor. The last thing you want to do is wait there with them, because you're pretty sure that you would then be exposed to at least a dozen diseases that are all much worse than what you have. You want to go somewhere else, anywhere else, to wait. But you would be making a BIG mistake. That's because there is no way to know which "number" the doctor is seeing at that time, so you have to constantly ask the stern-faced dragon lady at the desk how things are progressing. If you should leave and your number is called while you're away, you're in for a good tongue-lashing from Mrs. Dragon Lady upon your return. You will definitely not be next in line, but will possibly be punished by being put at the end of the line. At the very least several other patients will be allowed to go ahead of you.

Finally your long wait to see a doctor is rewarded. Your number is called. You press through the waiting throng into the doctor's office, only to discover that there are at least two doctors, and sometimes three or four, occupying the same small office. The doctors have their desks placed facing one another, which seems very friendly and a most economical use of space. It also means, however, that you sit on one side of the doctor and, sitting a foot or two away from you is another patient sitting alongside the other doctor. And the other patient may have his or her entire family, including all of his or her cousins, standing there to lend moral support. So if you should have a severe itch in the groin or a bad case of 'roids, you may decide to not tell the doctor your problem, lest everyone else in the room learn about your diagnosis. And the door to the doctor's office is never closed. There are always many people waiting at the entrance to get in. So you may have an audience of a few dozen people, seemingly all with their eyes fixed on you, waiting to hear what the foreigner has wrong with him.

So let's say that the doctor needs to examine you. You go to one side of the room. There's an examining table in a corner, onto which you hop. The doctor courteously draws a flimsy curtain around you to give you privacy. But there are still a dozen people right outside the curtain who can hear everything that's said.

Let's say you've endured this humiliation. You emerge, facing all the staring eyes fixed on you. The physician now says that he or she needs a sample of skin or blood, depending on your ailment. Or you have a stomach complaint and they need a urine or stool sample. The doctor then writes out something on another little flimsy piece of paper and hands it to you. Any Chinese person knows that you need to take this "document" to the laboratory, called in Chinese the "huàyànshì" ("hwah-yen-shure").

So you take your piece of paper and try to locate the lab, which may be on some other floor of the hospital entirely. You once again wade through a sea of people until you find the room that serves as the laboratory. You force your way in and give your precious slip of paper to another stern-faced woman, who looks like she went to the same charm school as the matron in the doctor's office. Now let's say they require a stool sample from you. The lab worker will immediately give you a small box made of paper in which you are to deposit your stool sample. For a urine sample you are given a little cup, much like in the States. The lab does not have its own designated facility for collecting samples, so you will need to find the nearest restroom. When you find the lavatory, you discover that it's inevitably a squat toilet. You get on your haunches and use the tiny paper-made box to squeeze your stool sample from your buttocks into the little container. It's a trick worthy of the finest contortionist and requires great precision. Often you're given a toothpick so you, and we're not kidding here, can skewer your stool sample from the toilet bowl, allowing you to pick it up and place it—like an hors d'oeuvre—in the box.

You put the lid on the little paper box and walk back to the lab. It's just one more humiliating moment after another as you walk past the crowd of waiting people with your stool sample in hand. Now it's time to wait again outside the lab for the results.

You will probably be called twenty or thirty minutes later and the results given to you on yet another piece of paper. You take the paper with the lab results back to your doctor.

Since you were gone the doctor has of course been seeing other patients, so once again you need to wait until the doctor will see you again. Now you become one of those onlookers whom you resented only moments before, listening in on other patients' problems. Eventually you are able to sit down again across from the doctor. He or she will inform you what illness you have and give you a prescription. Everything will be written down in the little booklet. The physician keeps no record at all of your diagnosis or your treatment. So hold onto that little booklet for your next visit to the hospital. Of course if you have some extensive test or operation, the hospital will keep a record of this, just as in a Western hospital.

You then take your prescription back to the lobby. Before going to the pharmacy in the hospital you must go to the "Accounts Window" ("huajiachu" or "hwah-geeah-choo"). Here they will calculate the cost of the medicine and demand that you pay first.

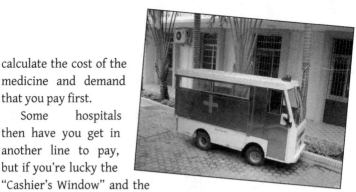

Some hospitals then have you get in another line to pay, but if you're lucky the "Cashier's Window" and the "Accounts Window" are one and the same.

You must pay cash, unless you are a Chinese person with an insurance policy that covers you. Foreigners always have to pay cash at these ordinary Chinese hospitals.

After you pay, your piece of paper with your prescription will be stamped. You then go to yet another line to pick up your medicine. Very likely by this time of the day, there is a long line at the cashier's window as well as at the pharmacy window.

If you just require one or two common medications, the pharmacist will probably gather them right away and throw them at you under the window. If there are a number of pre-scriptions to be filled, however, and especially if Chinese herbal medicines are required, you will need to wait. This wait can be as "short" as thirty minutes or as long as an hour or two. By this time, even if you showed up at the hospital at 7:30 in the morning, it may very well now be close to 5:00 in the afternoon.

Let's say you also need an injection in addition to the pre-scription. After you pay the money at the cashier's window in the lobby, you then go to the Inoculations Room with your receipt and get your shot. If you have a fever and they need to take your temperature, do not expect that they will simply stick a thermometer in your ear for a few seconds, as they now do in the States. No, it's the good old-fashioned mercury thermometer that we Baby Boomers knew back in our childhood.

There are reforms being enacted in the Chinese medical system in recent years, just as in every other aspect of Chinese life. But throughout the latter part of the twentieth century the above "day in the life of a Chinese outpatient" was common in all Chinese hospitals. You need to be prepared for this still, should you fall ill outside of one of the major cities in China. If you're unfortunate enough to go to a regular Chinese hospital as described above, prepare for that to be your activity for the entire day.

Be sure to check with your local health care professionals to find out what immunizations they might recommend for China. Although no shots are required for short-term stays, we particularly suggest you update your inoculations for hepatitis, which is a sufficient concern in the U.S. but which is extremely widespread in China.

Taking Along
the Basic Necessities

Since China's swift modernization in the past few decades, most of the products that we Westerners rely upon in our daily lives are now available in the Middle Kingdom.

If you forgot to pack your razor blades or hair spray or aspirin, you won't have much trouble finding a store in China where you can buy them. The four- and five-star hotels in China where the majority of us Westerners stay provide you with complimentary shampoo, toothpaste, and combs anyway. But there are a few things that you still better make sure you bring along from your home country, because you'll have a devil of a time finding them in China. The most critical example that springs to mind is deodorant.

Stinky Armpits and Other Hygiene Tales

Deodorant is an extremely commonplace item in countries like the U.S., where few people dare go out in public without anointing themselves under both armpits with the stuff in one form or another. Because a person's own natural body odor is generally not appreciated by his (and, sometimes, her) fellow human beings, deodorant helps keep our society on a civil footing by making it bearable to be with our neighbor at close quarters. In China, however, almost no one uses deodorant and it's nearly impossible to find it in any store other than large stores like Wal-Mart and Carrefour.

Chinese pharmacies, unlike their Western counterparts, do not carry products like shampoo or deodorant, but only medicine. Supermarkets in America always have a section for things like deodorant.

When Larry was coming perilously close to running out of deodorant on our last trip around China, we entered a fancy department store in a large Chinese city. We were confident that if they didn't have such a product, they would at least be able to direct us to some store that could save Qin's delicate sensibilities and hence save our marriage.

Even though Qin grew up in China and although we are both long-time professors of Chinese, we did not even know what the Chinese might call this invaluable elixir for preserving social harmony. The old phrase that Larry had learned in Taiwan three decades ago, namely "water for eliminating body odor," certainly didn't register with store clerks in today's mainland China. We explained that we wanted to buy some kind of cologne ("fragrant water" in Chinese) that you put under your arms to smell better. Most clerks would tell us simply that they had a vague notion of what we meant, but that their store definitely carried no such product. Finally one clerk told us that what we wanted was "tǐ xiāng shuǐ" ("tee-sheeang-shway" or "body fragrant water") and

that we could buy it at a British pharmacy across the street. Sure enough, when entering that pharmacy we breathed a sigh of relief as we spied the name Gillette on many of their products, including deodorant.

The point of all this is that, despite how modern cities like Beijing and Shanghai have become, you can often get lulled into a false sense of security (remember the section on bathrooms at the beginning of the book?). Don't take anything for granted, and do not always count on finding everything you might need. In places that are more off the beaten track, which are increasingly popular with Western tourists, shopping for what you might have left behind at home becomes all the more difficult. So besides making absolutely sure you have packed your own prescription medicines that you rely on, be sure to pack ordinary things like deodorant as well.

The following is a story that happened to a student group that Larry led on an adventurer's tour of China in 1984. It will help us emphasize that when you travel the globe, always make sure to carry with you the most essential items. You cannot depend on being able to pick them up just anywhere. This includes feminine hygiene products.

Back in the early 1980s one of the best places to go to see

China off the beaten path was the jungle area in southeastern Yunnan Province known as Xishuangbanna ("See-shwahng-bah-nah").

With a name that sounds a bit like "she swang banana," this lush area of banana trees and elephants lies near China's border with Laos and Burma. Somewhat sadly, this region is now completely developed for tourism, but back in the '80s few foreign tour groups ever visited this remote part of the country. Instead of the myriad hotels that now accommodate visitors, there was only one guesthouse acceptable to foreigners.

Larry thought it would be exciting to see what was then an unspoiled part of China, where the Dai minority people wore colorful costumes, lived in houses built on stilts, and farmed with water buffalo. In those days the fastest way to reach this area was to take a small twin-prop plane to the nearest city with an airport, then take a bus ride of around seven hours over hilly terrain to reach the small town from which the group planned to explore the surrounding jungle for the next three days.

Perhaps it was the Chinese tour guide's fault for not explaining more clearly to Larry about how the baggage for this trip was to be handled. Or perhaps Larry had not listened carefully enough to the guide's explanation when the two were drinking beer together the night before they embarked on this adventure. Whoever was to blame, Larry and his students did not realize that when the guide asked the American group to leave their suitcases outside their doors the next morning before departing their hotel in the provincial city of Kunming, they would not be seeing their luggage again for three days. Wasn't it obvious that neither the tiny twin-prop plane nor the minibus they would take to get to the jungle could possibly hold the large suitcases with which Westerners travel? Unfortunately, this was not at all obvious to Larry and his students.

Larry's group did not suspect anything was wrong until they had survived a bumpy plane ride on a plane that would have looked familiar to Baron von Richthofen, and found themselves on an even bumpier bus headed for the jungle area. One of Larry's female students suddenly turned to her teacher, whom she had always trusted, and asked, "Where is our luggage?" She had astutely noticed, you see, that the group's suitcases were not in the bus with them. "Oh, they're probably coming along behind us in another bus," Larry replied without total confidence. "No, they're not," piped up the Chinese guide. "They'll be waiting for you at the hotel in Kunming when we go back there three days from now." Larry's group suddenly turned surly. He realized how Captain Bligh must have felt when most of his crew on the *Bounty* turned against him.

After all, almost no one had anything with them except the clothes on their backs, their money, and their passports. The only one who had a clean change of underwear or even a toothbrush was Larry's friend, Norm. Norm had been all around the world and always made sure he had the bare essentials on his person at all times in a small tote bag.

Now it was the women in Larry's group who turned the most hostile. This was not due to the fact, as some of you men might hastily conclude, that in a crisis women are more excitable than men. No, it was because of an incredible coincidence: all of the women except Larry's sister, Nancy, were experiencing that once-a-month discomfort known euphemistically as a "period." It was one thing to be without a change of underwear or a toothbrush for three days. Underwear and other clothes could be washed out in the sink each night. You can at least rinse your mouth and use your fingers to clean your teeth. But to be without basic feminine hygiene items for three whole days was flat out asking too much of the women in Larry's long-suffering tour group. Remember that this was the same bunch of people who had needed to run for their lives to keep from being left behind in a village in the mountains of Sichuan Province.

"Don't panic, people," croaked the Captain Bligh of college tour groups. "Surely there will be a store on the way where you can buy what you need," Larry said to comfort the upset ladies.

"There isn't any town where we're headed, only a small village," cautioned the Chinese guide. For the next five hours or so it was very quiet on the bus as the women sulked and Larry vowed to lock his door securely that night to keep from being lynched. Finally the bus came within sight of a small group of stalls set up alongside the road, where they sold a variety of merchandise. Larry asked the driver to stop there so that they could attempt to buy something—anything that would help the women. Accompanied by his oldest female student, Larry went up to the minority women who were in charge of these roadside stalls.

There they discovered toothbrushes, toothpaste, soap, towels—all the things they most craved at this point. Was it too much to hope they would also have feminine napkins? When Larry explained to these minority women that the ladies in his group were having their period, the Dai women immediately grasped the situation. They took out a large amount of what looked to Larry like pink crepe paper and handed it to him.

Larry's female student was totally at a loss as to how to use this crepe paper to solve her problem. The Dai women explained that women in China knew how to use string to keep the paper in its intended place. Larry asked that they be so kind as to pantomime to his student how to do this, while he beat a hasty retreat to the bus. The Dai women willingly obliged. Larry and his other students watched from the bus as the minority women showed Larry's student how to create a maxi-pad: Chinese style. When the woman student returned to the bus and they drove away, waving a thank-you to the Dai women, the Americans could not help but notice that the minority women were not just smiling but were convulsed with laughter at the seeming insanity of it all: these strange foreigners who had dropped in out of nowhere, asking for a lesson in how to use feminine napkins!

Equipped with enough crepe paper to decorate a hundred bicycles for a Fourth of July parade, the women in Larry's group were able to make it through the next three days. His students' dignity and clothing (not to mention Larry's life) were all saved.

Travel Troubles and Startling Snafus

Whenever you travel anywhere in the world you have to be ready to expect the unexpected. A train might be late, or your plane can't take off because of bad weather, or you end up losing your luggage. A tourist just has to be able to roll with the punches, knowing that very likely sooner or later something unforeseen might pop up. If that is true when traveling around America or France, it is even truer when visiting a developing nation like China.

Flight Fiasco

The travel troubles that we described in a few previous tales of woe were from more than two decades ago, when China was much more backward and the travel infrastructure much more primitive. Surely in the summer of 2010 my wife and I would have no trouble in flying from Beijing to Shanghai. After all, we would be departing from the newly renovated Capital Airport and traveling between China's two largest and most important cities. It was a flight we had taken often, so we knew well that it was a mere two hours from takeoff to landing. But we had forgotten that when you travel, especially in China, you should always expect the unexpected. Even in 2010. Even in Beijing!

Our plane was scheduled to depart at 9:30 in the morning. It takes fifty minutes to an hour to make it from downtown Beijing, where we were staying, to the airport. And it's always advisable to arrive two hours before a domestic flight, as the airlines never tire of reminding us. So we forced ourselves to get up at 5:30 in the morning, were at the front desk to check out by 6:00 A.M., and even after the customary wait for the maids to scour our room for signs of petty theft, were in a cab and on the way to the airport by 6:30 A.M. Our driver made excellent time, and we arrived by 7:10, more than two hours before our imminent departure.

We entered the immense airport and checked in with no problem, but when we went through the security area, all the lights in the building momentarily dimmed. We overheard the employees say to one another that the dimming of the lights was likely due to thunder and lightning going on outside.

Yet when we entered the airport just moments before, there was no hint of rain.

Even though it was still nearly two hours before our flight was to leave, we proceeded to our gate. Perhaps we could catch a few Z's while we waited. On our way we heard the discouraging announcement that all flights had stopped boarding because of thunder and lightning. We then discovered that our gate was not one of the dozens on the upper levels of the airport, with relatively capacious seating areas. In spite of the fact that our flight was on a major airline between the two largest cities in China, our gate was on the very lowest level of the place, in a fairly tiny basement area with just a few gates and only around thirty seats.

The problem was that so many flights had stopped boarding that almost every inch of space down below was taken up by people and their carry-on luggage. Not only was every seat taken, but there were dozens of people sitting on the ground. Others were frantically trying to get to the small counter to ask the airline employees when their flight might take off or to get a glimpse of the one small screen with flight departure information. The scene was reminiscent of the fall of Saigon, with the same sense of urgency and chaos, only in miniature. It didn't help that in Chinese airports there are often no announcements as to flight delays or, for that matter, boarding announcements for domestic flights.

When Larry managed to eventually work his way through the crowd to get a look at the screen with flight information, there was absolutely no estimate given for the new departure times for any of the flights. The word "delay" did not even appear on the screen. Nor was there the slightest information forthcoming from the seemingly clueless airline employees behind the desk. The one thing that Larry was able to determine was that there were three flights ahead of ours scheduled to leave from that same gate. Since there was no place to sit down in the bowels of the airport near our gate, we took the escalator up a few flights and found some comfortable seats in which to wait out the delay. Our plan was that by 9:00 A.M., a half hour before our flight was

supposed to leave, Larry would pop downstairs and see what the situation was. We would definitely not be able to hear any announcements about flights leaving from our gate in the basement area from two floors up, even if the airlines were to make such an announcement. When we looked out the large windows upstairs we could see that outside it had begun to rain, but only lightly. No sound of thunder and no sign of lightning. Nothing to cause any major delays at such a huge and modern airport as the Beijing Capital Airport.

When Larry did descend the escalator at 9:00 A.M. to see what was going on, we couldn't help but notice that by now it was pouring rain outside. Down below, in what appeared more and more to be the lowest deck of the *Titanic*, nothing had changed. Except that perhaps there were even more disgruntled and hopeless looking Chinese people standing or sitting there, all equally discouraged. There were a few Western tourists, too, who looked even more hopeless, since they couldn't speak Chinese and so couldn't commiserate or share information with other passengers.

Finally, by 10:30, all of a sudden and with no announcement, people began to rush through the gate to get on the buses waiting outside that would take them to their planes. People leaving on the flights before ours had already boarded and, in spite of the lack of announcements, Larry could see that our flight would board next. But given the lack of information, we had no idea exactly when our turn would come. Qin decided that there would surely be time for her to visit the bathroom upstairs. And there seemed little hope that our flight would board any time soon. But a few moments after she left, there was a stampede of people rushing toward the gate. Our flight was finally boarding, and Qin was nowhere in sight!

She finally appeared just as it seemed the bus outside was about to be filled to capacity. We hurried through the gate and onto the bus. We had to wait for about five minutes in the stifling summer heat, but we finally rode the minute or two to our plane. The other passengers, in typical Chinese manner, did not make any attempt to line up, but pushed and shoved to get up the stairs and onto the plane.

By around 11:00 A.M., an hour and a half after we were scheduled to depart, our plane finally took off.

We could sit back and relax, thinking that in two hours we would be in Shanghai. But after flying for an hour and fifteen minutes, the captain suddenly announced that due to lightning in Shanghai, we would be unable to proceed there. Instead we would be landing in Dalian in fifteen minutes. Dalian is directly east of Beijing, whereas Shanghai is southeast of the capital, with the emphasis on south! This would be like taking a flight from Chicago to Atlanta and, shortly before you were scheduled to arrive, being told with no prior warning that you would be landing in Newark instead. That means that the captain had known for at least a half hour or more that we would not be going to Shanghai after all, but had not thought it important to share that information with us.

Interestingly, there was only a slight groan from the passengers at the pilot's announcement. We landed in Dalian, where the weather was very fine, indeed. We waited and waited in the plane at the Dalian Airport, with no news forthcoming. When we discovered we had to remain in that metal box on the tarmac for many hours, Qin recalled horror stories she had read about passengers in China being kept on a plane on the tarmac for as many as eight hours, with water running out but not allowed to leave. Now we were in that same situation! Amazingly, the Chinese passengers still did not complain, either to the flight attendants or to each other. Many got on their cell phones to tell friends and family that they were delayed, with no idea as to when they would arrive, but no complaints to the flight attendants. The passengers were agitated, but didn't seem to care that no updates were given. China is not a society where people are accustomed to being informed by the authorities as to what is happening.

During the five-and-a-half hours that we were waiting, only once were we given any water, and only a half-cup of water at that. They also gave us a small Chinese sandwich, made with dried flatbread wrapped around a small piece of meat of uncertain origin. By 3:00 P.M. some people started to give up hope of ever reaching our destination. They began to ask the beautiful, tall, and slender but clearly hassled female flight attendants as to when we would be leaving for Shanghai. Every time these patient women apologized for the delay, but they  had no information and clearly were as clueless as we were. In order to placate the passengers, the attendants gave each of us a small bag of chocolate cookies. But they gave us no water to wash them down!

The captain only came on over the intercom three times. The first two times it was merely to tell us that he had no information from the air control tower, but that as soon as he had such information, he would pass it on to us. Very helpful, indeed! The last time the captain came on, he announced that the air control tower had not informed him when we could leave, but he assured us that we would be continuing on. At this, everyone on the plane laughed. That was because the captain seemed to imply that we would eventually be on our way to somewhere, but he didn't say where that might be!

The most frustrating thing for us as foreign tourists was the total lack of any information forthcoming from the cockpit. If this had been the U.S., the pilot would have come on every ten or fifteen minutes to give us an update on our situation. After several hours of waiting, we would most likely have been allowed to deplane and wait in the airport lounge until we were ready to take off. But this was China.

All of a sudden around 5:30 P.M., just after we were thinking about where we might find lodging in Dalian, the captain announced over the intercom that the flight attendants should prepare for takeoff. Everyone on the plane immediately buckled up. Chinese people are not used to obeying rules, but they are used to obeying authority! In spite of having to wait for over five hours with no news from the pilot, when the captain said, "prepare for departure," like sheep everyone instantly snapped to attention. Only Qin asked one of the flight attendants in an ironic tone exactly where we were going this time. The attendant smiled knowingly and assured her that this time we would be going to our desired destination. None of the Chinese passengers outside of Qin would think to question authority like that. But Qin has lived in the U.S. for twenty-five years!

We didn't take off for another fifteen minutes, but there finally was a sense that we all might get to see Shanghai after all, even if it were for a late dinner rather than an early lunch! We did arrive at the Shanghai Airport, where it was already dark, only eight hours later than scheduled. Except for us, none of the passengers grumbled or complained as we arrived. They had been given chocolate cookies, after all!

What Reservations?!

When we make flight or hotel reservations, we expect those reservations to be honored. That's especially true when we've already paid for those flights or hotel rooms. While this is generally a valid assumption in China, we have experienced as many as three occasions on recent trips where we were unpleasantly surprised to find that our reservations, paid for ahead of time, did us no good whatsoever. We present these as cautionary tales, so that you will not be completely shocked or unprepared should something like this happen to you.

The first tale of woe, and by far the most traumatic, occurred on our most recent trip.

We had just spent several days in the beautiful mountain resort area of Lushan, which we had to leave abruptly to take Qin to the hospital in Jiujiang. You might remember that story from the chapter on Medical Emergencies. We had booked two tickets to fly from Jiujiang to Beijing. Almost everything on our trip had been arranged by CITS, the China International Travel Service, through whom almost all foreigners book their travel in China. CITS had booked a great many trips to China for us in the past, and had always done very well by us. As usual, we had paid for all hotels, as well as all domestic travel, months before our trip. That included the Jiujiang to Beijing flight. The only things we had to pay for on this trip were our meals, local transportation such as taxis and subways, and a few fees to enter certain villages or scenic areas. The day we were to fly out of Jiujiang for Beijing was at the end of our trip, less than forty-eight hours from the time we would get on a plane in Beijing to return to the U.S. We expected we'd only need to spend a little more Chinese money to pay for a few meals in Beijing and the taxi ride to the airport there. But just to be on the safe side, some days previous we had exchanged money once again to get an extra few thousand yuan. That ended up being a godsend at the Jiujiang airport, as it turned out.

Our flight from Jiujiang to Beijing wasn't scheduled to depart until 9:05 P.M. Our very likable young CITS guide and his equally amiable driver picked us up at our hotel 2½ hours before the flight and drove us to the airport, about forty-five minutes away. The guide assured us that this would allow plenty of time for check-in. This turned out to be an understatement. Although Jiujiang is a city of 1.5 million people, the airport consists of but two counters and two gates, with only six flights departing each day. The waiting room is just one very large, barren hall. When our car pulled up to the airport, there were no cars at all parked in front, and no one waiting inside. We even began to doubt whether there really was a flight scheduled to leave the airport that evening. But we were assured when we saw the electronic sign over the counter announcing a flight leaving for Beijing at 9:05 P.M. We were all the more assured when we saw four other passengers eventually arrive with their luggage and take most of the remaining seats in the waiting area.

Several days before our flight we had asked our guide whether he had our tickets for this flight. He had told us that no tickets were necessary. Everything at Chinese airports was so up-to-date that all reservations for domestic flights were now on computer. All we needed to do, he assured us, was to show our passports at the check-in counter and all would be well. This was a bit worrisome to us, since in the past and as recently as the year before, someone from CITS or our guide had always given us actual paper tickets for all our flights. But CITS and their excellent guides had never let us down, and when we arrived at the Jiujiang airport, the guide asserted once again that our tickets were on computer and all was arranged. Since the driver's wife had called not once but three times during our trip to the airport to find out when her husband was coming home for dinner, the guide apologetically told us that he and the driver would be leaving us at the airport before the check-in for our flight. But we had nothing to worry about, he repeated. We said our genuinely warm goodbyes and our only friends in Jiujiang left us there in the waiting room of the airport. In the past, whenever we had the luxury of a guide who took us to the airport, he or she would always wait until we had checked in for our flight before leaving us. But who were we to endanger the marital happiness of our driver, or delay his dinner any more than we already had with our extremely late departure time?

So we were alone, but looking forward to returning to Beijing, where the next morning Qin could obtain the kind of superior medical attention she urgently required. If you'll remember from the chapter on Medical Emergencies, she was really suffering from a serious intestinal bug that the physicians of Jiujiang were unable to cure. She was weak from having eaten next to nothing for the previous five days, but had summoned up her last bit of strength in order to make it back to "civilization" in Beijing.

We sat for a good half hour in the waiting room until five minutes before the counter was scheduled to open for check-in. At that point we hurriedly rolled our suitcases over to the counter, to be the first in line when the staff should appear to check our bags and give us our boarding passes. Even in this airport that only had six flights a day, the electronic sign then announced a twenty-minute delay in check-in and departure times, but no matter. We would just stand there twenty minutes longer, knowing that within a few hours we would be back in Qin's hometown of Beijing, home to the kind of excellent medical facilities she was so anxious to avail herself of.

Up to this point in our trip, it was always Qin, as native speaker, who would handle things like this. But since she was feeling so poorly, she told Larry that it was about time he took charge. After all, he was fluent in Chinese and should have the practice of handling the check-in procedure in Mandarin. When check-in finally began, Larry quickly and confidently approached the woman at the counter and presented our passports. She asked for our tickets and Larry told her that CITS had reserved two seats for us, as she would readily see on her computer screen. The woman at the counter looked over the list of passengers, glanced once more at our passports, and informed us that our names were not on the list. At this point Qin, who was desperate to get out of Jiujiang, and knowing this was the last flight out that day, rushed up to the counter and insisted that the woman was probably not spelling our name, Herzberg, correctly. The woman typed in our name again: H-E-R-Z-B-E-R-G. Nope, there were no seats reserved for any Herzbergs, or any other foreigners, for that matter, regardless of how the name was spelled.

Qin insisted that CITS had made the reservations for us. The woman responded that this mattered little, since nothing showed up on computer. She asked what our confirmation number was, to which Qin replied, exasperated, that there was no way we would know that, since we were not the ones to make the reservation. Did we have a cell phone, the woman asked. We could call our guide to find out the reservation number, she suggested. The woman was shocked to learn that we had no cell phone, particularly because everyone, but everyone, has a cell phone in China today.

Lesson Number One: bring a Smart Phone to China with you and keep it handy!

"What are we supposed to do?!" asked Qin. "We have to be on that flight!" Qin then gave the woman the cell phone number of our guide, which we had at least been wise enough to keep, and pleaded with her to call the guide to set things straight. In the meantime, though, we had to remove our very heavy suitcases from the conveyor belt on which Larry had already placed them and go to the back of the line at the head of which we had stood so smugly just moments before.

The woman left her subordinate to check in the rest of the passengers, all of whom were Chinese and all of whom had tickets in hand and were able to check in with absolutely no problem.

She was as good as her word, though, and did manage to reach our guide. She called Qin over to the phone to speak to the guide, in front of another line of passengers checking in for the only other flight leaving the airport that night, this one for Guangzhou. The guide gave Qin the bad news that he did not know the confirmation number for our reservation, since it was the central CITS office in Beijing that had made all our travel arrangements. It was those folks who would know our confirmation number, not he.

By this time it was 8:30 at night and, of course, the CITS office in Beijing would be closed. The woman at the counter, while not exactly sympathetic with our plight, nevertheless continued to try to resolve our problem. We asked if there were still empty seats on the flight. She told us that fortunately there were still some seats available. The only thing we could do, she told us, was to purchase two tickets, and pointed to a far-off counter where a man was seated in the semi-darkness, completely idle in that tiny airport. With only ten minutes left before the plane was scheduled to begin boarding, we raced over to the man to buy the tickets. How much would it cost, we asked him. 2,700 yuan, he replied.

Now, 2,700 yuan is almost exactly US$450! That was far more than we had expected, and certainly much more than the price that CITS had paid for the tickets. But we were buying these tickets at the last minute at the airport, without any recourse to discounts given to travel agencies like CITS.

Would they accept a foreign credit card? Absolutely not! This was not the Beijing, Shanghai, or Guangzhou airport, but a tiny airport in a much smaller city. The problem was that we weren't sure we had that much Chinese money left in our wallets! We hurriedly counted our money, to discover that miraculously we had just a little over 3,000 yuan. We could afford to pay for the tickets, although this would leave us barely enough money to take a cab to our hotel from the airport in Beijing. When we insisted that reservations had been made for our flight, the man checked the computer screen and told us that, yes, reservations had originally been made in our names. But since CITS had not confirmed the flights, the reservations had been canceled!

Furious that we would have to pay for our plane tickets twice, and the second time pay 50-100% more than the original cost, Qin asked if the man at the counter would be so kind as to call the cell phone of our contact person for CITS in Beijing. Qin had been wise enough to ask the CITS office in the U.S., through our local travel agent, for the name, in both Chinese and English, as well as the contact phone numbers for some individual in the central office in Beijing who would be responsible for looking after us on our trip, should we encounter any problem. We had learned the importance of this when Larry had his foot broken by a mad bicyclist in Shanghai and we needed to suddenly change our travel plans.

Cautious Qin had wisely kept handy the contact information

for the man in the CITS office in Beijing. The man at the counter, who was waiting for us to pay the 2,700 yuan for our tickets, amazingly was kind enough to dial the cell phone number of our contact person. No luck, the man at the counter then told us. Our contact person had turned off his cell! By this time Qin was perspiring profusely, weak and tired as she was from being sick, and now all in an understandable tizzy over this shocking turn of events.

A minute later the cell phone of the man at the counter rang. Great, we thought! He's now going to take a personal call and we'll miss our flight! To our great surprise, it was the man in Beijing calling and asking for Qin!! Qin blurted out our problem, but our man in Beijing apologetically explained that there was nothing he could do at that point. We would have to purchase the tickets. He would, however, refund the full 2,700 yuan to us once we arrived in Beijing.

Lesson Number Two: If you're traveling on your own, rather than as a member of a group, make sure that your travel agency gives you the name and cell phone number of a contact person in China who will be personally responsible for you during your trip. Even if that person can't resolve every issue on the spot, you will at least get some restitution when this sort of problem occurs.

The plane to Beijing was soon scheduled to board and we still had no tickets. Nor had we checked our considerable amount of luggage. With blazing speed we paid for our tickets and Larry rushed over to the counter, where no one remained except for the woman who had originally waited on us. Larry handed over the hard-won tickets and hurriedly hoisted the bags onto the conveyor belt.

When Larry apologized for having troubled her so much, the woman quickly softened and explained that this sort of thing happened all the time!

Our two large suitcases were so heavy that they greatly exceeded the allowable limit of 20 kilograms per bag. By all rights we should have had to pay a 450–500 yuan penalty. This would have pretty much exhausted all the money we had left. It was very possible we wouldn't be able to pay for a cab to our hotel once we arrived in Beijing! The woman behind the counter mercifully let our bags roll down the conveyor belt without saying a word. Perhaps she realized we had already been through enough of an ordeal. Or perhaps she just didn't want to hold up our flight. In any case, she handed over the boarding passes and, bags checked, we headed off to the waiting room to await the boarding of our flight.

Qin's heart had finally stopped beating at twice the normal rate and we plopped down in the waiting room, relieved that we would be on that flight to Beijing after all. Proper medical attention was only 12 hours away. We chatted about all the things we hoped to do in Beijing the next day after Qin had seen a doctor, including saying goodbye to friends, shopping for Chinese pastries to take back home, and packing our bags. Suddenly several young women who worked at the airport rushed up to inform us that we were waiting in the wrong waiting room. There were only two waiting rooms, and we were sitting in the one for passengers waiting for the flight to Guangzhou. The other waiting room, which is where passengers for the flight to Beijing were supposed to wait, was now empty. That was because all the passengers going to Beijing had already boarded the plane! In our relief on obtaining tickets to Beijing, we had neglected to take note of which waiting room we were supposed to be waiting in.

Back in panic mode, we raced to the other waiting room and out the door to the runway, dragging our two small carry-on suitcases behind us. In a tiny airport like that in Jiujiang, passengers must make a long walk out on the runway to the plane, and climb up the long flight of metal steps to board.

Ill as Qin was feeling, it was incredible how fast she was able to run to the plane and scamper up the steps to get on board! Of course our seats had to be at the very back of the plane, so that all the passengers could watch us rush on and dash madly past every single row to get seated for take-off.

During the two-hour flight to Beijing we were able to recover our composure. Nevertheless, we wouldn't arrive in Beijing until around 11:30 at night, where we would need to claim our checked luggage and find a taxi to take us the forty-five minutes or so to our hotel. So there were a few more hoops through which to jump before we would be able to get into a nice bed and sleep off the day's adventures.

It was nearly midnight before we had grabbed our suitcases off the carousel and were ready to leave the airport. At the exit to the baggage claim area there was the usual crowd of people waiting for the arriving passengers. And, as usual, some in the crowd were holding signs with the names of the businessmen or tourists they were there to pick up. To our surprise, there was a friendly looking man standing there holding up a sign with our names on it! It seems that our CITS contact person in Beijing had been the one who should have confirmed our reservations on the flight from Jiujiang. He was truly a very nice and kind man, who felt terrible that we had been so inconvenienced by his uncharacteristic mistake. He had, therefore, ordered one of his assistants to pick us up at the airport, along with a car and driver, to take us to our hotel. And this at midnight, when the assistant and the driver had every right to be in bed! This unexpected helper, who had miraculously appeared like an angel, grabbed the largest suitcase and led us to the waiting car. During the ride to our hotel, our new friend took out his wallet and handed over to us the 2,700 yuan we had spent for our airplane tickets.

Lesson Number Three: CITS is really a wonderful travel organization. In the fifteen trips around China they have arranged for us or for Larry and his students, they have never before made any mistakes. But when they do, you can be sure they will make every effort to make restitution. Nevertheless,

Lesson Number Four: If you are traveling solo, when you arrive in China ask CITS, or whatever travel organization makes your travel arrangements, to be sure to confirm any flights you are scheduled to take!

Our plane tickets from Jiujiang to Beijing were not the only reservation that wasn't honored during that same trip. When arranging our trip months earlier, we had asked CITS to reserve us a room in the five-star Yangzhou Guest House for a three-night stay. From our research online, we had discovered that the city of Yangzhou, not far from Nanjing, is a little-known, if historically famous, gem of a place. We also learned that the Yangzhou Guest House is the best hotel in town. The rooms are very comfortable, and the hotel sits on five beautiful acres of trees, flowers, and ponds. It's also within an easy walk from the absolutely lovely and tranquil "Slender West Lake" park, a very large and beautifully laid out scenic treasure with a great variety of wildlife, greenery, and small lakes. We were really looking forward to our stay in the Yangzhou Guest House, which formerly was open only to Chinese officials but was now open to the general public for a few months each year.

All of our reservations for this trip were made through CITS months ahead of time. The CITS office in San Francisco had sent us a long e-mail confirming each and every one the week before we left for China.

Very early in the morning of the second day after we arrived in Beijing, the first stop on our itinerary, a representative from the CITS office dropped by our hotel to give us the train tickets to Shanghai, from where we would travel to Yangzhou two days after that. He explained to us that in spite of our long-standing reservation, we would no longer be able to stay at the Yangzhou Guest House. It seems that the local officials in the city had just commandeered the entire hotel for a "meeting," i.e., free vacation at the taxpayers' expense, complete with wine, women, and big feasts. He could not tell us what alternate plan they now had for our stay. When the CITS office opened later that morning, we were to phone his boss, who would explain everything.

We were really upset! Not only had we been looking forward for many months to being able to stay at such a special hotel as the Yangzhou Guest House, but our visit to Yangzhou was less than a week away and we didn't know where we would be laying our heads when we got there! We were aware from previous experience that a hotel reservation in China might be canceled only days ahead, if the local officials decide they want to "meet" there. This is only a problem when the hotel in question is one of the best in town and has a prime location. On another trip only a few years before, we had been bumped from the hotel we had reserved in Shanghai, right by the Bund. The Party officials had commandeered all the better hotels in that area, in order to enjoy the World Expo taking place in the city at that time, and all reservations previously made for those days were canceled. CITS had told us they, too, were unhappy about this but were powerless to challenge the local government. They had found us an equally nice hotel, albeit nowhere close to the Bund. And now, once again, we were being bumped from our hotel at the last minute.

Promptly at 9:00 A.M., when the CITS office was scheduled to open, Larry would call the number of our contact person there. Larry was all ready to read him the riot act. Not a confrontational person, he was determined this time to assert his rights. "This kind of thing would never happen in the U.S. or any other developed nation!" he would declare. "A reservation is a contract between the hotel and the guest, and should be honored just as a legal contract would be!" Larry was all set to demand a room at the next best hotel in Yangzhou as well as a refund of the difference in price between the Guest House and whatever lesser hotel they might now put us in.

At 9:00 A.M., armed with his prepared speech, Larry phoned the CITS representative. The line was busy!

A moment later our hotel phone rang. It was our contact person. His line had been busy because he had been trying to call us. His English name was Charming, and he certainly lived up to his chosen moniker. Before Larry could launch into his diatribe, Charming hastily apologized for this unfortunate turn of events. He, too, was angry that Chinese government officials could do something like this.

However, things were not as bad as we had been led to believe. We would be able to stay at the Yangzhou Guest House after all, at least for the second and third nights of our stay in the city. It was only for the first night they they would have to put us in another hotel. Charming assured us that this hotel was also a five-star hotel and in the same neighborhood as the Guest House, if nowhere as close to "Slender West Lake." This gentleman from CITS was so charming and kind that any angry words on Larry's part seemed completely uncalled for.

When we arrived in Yangzhou, we discovered that the hotel CITS arranged for us for that first night in the city was very fine, indeed. And the staff was among the most accommodating and friendliest of any we had experienced in the more than a hundred hotel stays we have made in China.

Nevertheless, be forewarned: Should you book a room in a great location in one of the better hotels in China, you may have your reservations canceled on very short notice when the local officials decide to party there!

Holiday Crush: When Not to Visit China

Almost everywhere you go in China seems, as the Chinese put it, "a mountain of people, a sea of people." That is far truer during the major holidays, which are definitely not the time to visit the Middle Kingdom. We already told you that walking down the streets in a Chinese city or shopping in the stores on an ordinary day feels like Black Friday in the U.S. Now multiply that a hundredfold and you get a picture of the holiday scene in China. Among the busiest of travel times is around National Day, October 1, which commemorates the establishment of the People's Republic of China on that date in 1949. Since all Chinese people get more than a week off at this time, often including the weekends before and after National Day, almost everyone heads back

to their hometowns to see their loved ones. In a country that has seen more than 200 million people move from the countryside or small towns into the big cities, leaving behind the very young and the very old, most of those same 200 million people now want to return to the villages and towns to see the members of the family they left behind. Don't even consider visiting China between September 29 and October 7, or you will be swept away in a sea of people.

Another time to avoid traveling to China is during the Chinese New Year or "Spring Festival."

As most of you are aware, the Chinese New Year is based on the lunar calendar and therefore, depending on the year, falls sometime between late January and early February.

Although the holiday officially lasts only three days, most people take at least a week off at this time. For the ever larger percentage of Chinese who work for private companies, the Spring Festival can become as long as a fifteen-day vacation, since many employers want to allow their workers to travel across the country to reunite with their families. According to government statistics, in 2013 during the "Spring Festival" as many as 740 million plane, train, and bus tickets were purchased!

Staying away from China at these holiday times is not just

to avoid giant crowds of people. The tourist crush will make it impossible to get plane or train tickets, unless you've reserved them many months in advance. Hotels will also be booked solid, and you'll have a long wait to get a table in almost any restaurant. And, of course, every tourist site is jammed with people, including the scenic mountain resorts where you hope in vain to enjoy the peace and beauty of nature.

Other times when it's best to stay out of China, including a few days on either side, are:

- Tomb Sweeping Day, the Chinese Memorial Day, on the 15th day after the spring solstice, around April 5.
- May 1, International Labor Day, similar to the American Labor Day
- The Dragon Boat Festival, celebrated on the 5th day of the 5th month of the Chinese lunar calendar, which can fall anywhere between June 6 and June 23 in the solar calendar
- The Mid-Autumn Festival, similar to the American or Canadian Thanksgiving, celebrated on the 15th day of the 8th month of the lunar calendar, which depending on the year can fall anywhere between late September and early October

Eliminating all these 45 days as possibilities, that still leaves 320 days each year when you might plan a China visit!

13

The People

We've spent a good part of this book complaining about the seemingly rude behavior of the Chinese people. Even though we understand some of the reasons why the Chinese act the way they do, namely that they live everyday in an overcrowded society where the average educational level is still very low, that doesn't make it any less aggravating when they cut in line or fail in the social niceties. And yet when our American friends return from a stay in China, whether it's a two-week trip or a long sojourn there, they invariably say that what they enjoyed most about the entire experience was "the people." They really like the Chinese people whom they had a chance to get to know. "The historical sites, the scenery, the food, everything was great. But most of all we really liked the Chinese people. They were so friendly, good-humored, and welcoming." This very positive reaction of our friends doesn't seem to jibe at all with the quite negative impression we've given so far of the Chinese in certain social situations. What, then, accounts for this seeming disparity?

The reason is that there are probably few societies in the world that act in such a Jekyll-and-Hyde manner as the Chinese.

When we ask our educated Chinese friends why their fellow Chinese are so rude in public situations, they all agree that in China there are two standards of conduct or morality in your relationships with other people. There is one code of conduct that the Chinese use in dealing with people they know and a completely different one for dealing with strangers—not foreigners, per se, but rather within the constantly turning wheels of society as a whole.

There are not many cultures in the world where people look out for their family members the way the Chinese do. In every country in the world parents make great sacrifices to give their children a better life. Not only is this very true in China, but more than in most societies the children in turn reciprocate later in life by making terrific sacrifices for their parents. After all, this is the country of "filial piety," where children are expected to go to any lengths to serve their parents in return for the gift of life that they enjoy. In the modern world the Chinese and the other peoples of East Asia assume a much bigger role in taking care of their aged parents than do people in the West, for whom retirement homes are the most common solution.

In addition, arguably no other culture in the world puts such a premium on friendship as do the Chinese. Friendship was one of the five sacred Confucian relationships, which have been stressed by Chinese society over the past 2,500 years.

Chinese will do almost anything for their friends, sometimes at great financial and personal sacrifice to themselves.

When it seemed that Qin's mother, who lived in Beijing,

might need an extremely costly heart bypass procedure, the doctors insisted on having the Chinese equivalent of US$10,000 in cash before they would operate. We could send a check for that amount but it would take a month for the check to be approved and cashed. We turned to our Chinese friends in Beijing for help, asking them to loan us the money. Given the fact that the average Chinese income at that time was one-thirtieth that of the average American, US$10,000 was an astronomical amount of money for them to put together in just a few days. It would literally be like asking your American friends to loan you almost one hundred thousand dollars for an operation for your mother, with you promising to pay them back in a month. Two of Qin's friends pooled their resources and donated all their savings to loan us this money to try to save the life of Qin's mother. Fortunately for everyone (Qin's mother especially), the surgery was not needed after all, and the money was returned. But Qin's friends did not hesitate in offering immediate assistance, even if it meant spending every penny they had.

In China there is a very high standard of conduct, indeed, when it comes to taking care of friends and family. The same care and concern the Chinese show toward friends and family are also evident in their dealings with the foreign tourists and business associates whom they host. When you come to China as a member of a tourist group or business delegation, your Chinese hosts or guides will treat you as an honored guest.

You are not a nameless, faceless person on the street. You are someone who is important to them and for whom they are responsible. So they will not only be polite to you, they will go out of their way to help you in any way possible. In part it's because they want your business, but in part it's because this is traditional Chinese hospitality.

When you venture out on the street on your own, however, you become a faceless and nameless person. Even as a foreigner, you are just another obstacle for the Chinese, who must deal all day long with the constant press and push of people in their effort to get where they need to go and do what they need to do. Just when you're fed up with being bruised and buffeted around by the Chinese crowds, you walk into some place where the Chinese know you, and are touched by how friendly they are and at the interest they show toward you. That's because if you take even a few minutes to chat with the average Chinese person and get to know him or her just a little, most of the time you will find that they will then be very friendly and likeable indeed. If you make the effort to truly make friends with a Chinese person over a long period of time, you will never know a truer friend.

In the next chapter we deal with Chinese etiquette. Based on the early chapters in the book, we probably gave you the impression that the Chinese know nothing about etiquette or manners whatsoever. But there are many unspoken cultural rules

about proper behavior when it comes to dealing with people whom you know. The Chinese will generally obey these unwritten rules of conduct we outline in the next chapter when dealing with you, the foreign tourist or business person, just as they would with their friends and family members. You must recognize these rules and follow them in turn when dealing with the Chinese with whom you have meaningful contact. Leave the rules of the jungle that we have outlined in previous chapters for the jungle out on the streets. Let's now consider the Chinese at their civilized best.

14
A Basic Guide to Chinese Etiquette

Generally, the Chinese are quite informal people, much like Americans. Imagine a scale of one to ten to measure the spectrum of a culture's etiquette, with ten being at the extreme of, say, British aristocracy of the Victorian era, and one being John Belushi as Bluto in *Animal House*. In general, Japan would probably rate a 10, England an 8, China a 3, and America, believe it or not, probably around a 6 or so. In discussing Chinese etiquette, we're not talking about the total lack of manners displayed by Chinese people on the street to people they don't know. We're talking about the etiquette in the Chinese business world as well as in the world of Chinese friendships. The Chinese system of etiquette is very subtle and often the visual clues are very hard to spot.

Below is a long list of "dos" and "don'ts." These are the basic rules for how to behave properly when doing business or interacting with your Chinese friends.

Meeting and Greeting People

Use a person's full name, never just their given name, when

you meet them for the first time. In China as in most East Asian countries, a person's surname, or family name, is usually said first, followed by the given name. This naming convention can sometimes be confusing. In the West, for example, we have become accustomed to seeing many Japanese names run in the familiar "Westernized" first-name, last-name convention, such as Akira Kurosawa, or Toshiro Mifune, when in fact in Japan it would be Kurosawa Akira or Mifune Toshiro. A lot of Westerners still don't realize that Chinese basketball superstar Yao Ming's surname is Yao. The vast majority of Chinese still use three characters in their name: The surname is one character and the given name is two characters. There are still rare two-character surnames, such as Ouyang ("Ohyang") and Szto ("Sigh-toe"), but these are usually found in the south of China. Someone will hand you their business card and you will see three Chinese characters. Underneath (or on the back of the card) is usually written in English letters the person's name using the Chinese pinyin form of Romanization. For example, a man who is called Li Guoming is Mr. Li. When Romanized, the given name is usually written together as a single word, which is an immediate clue that Li, is, in fact the surname of the above gentleman. The more Chinese people you meet, the more you will get a feel for the many varieties of surnames out there. After a while, you will not only be able to figure out what a person's surname is based on the characters in their name, but, in some cases, also whether the person is a man or a woman. To confuse things a bit, however, these days some Chinese who are aware of our customs when meeting foreigners will give their name in the Western fashion, with their given name first. In these instances it is best to ask them for clarification as to which is their surname.

When doing business or cultural exchanges in China, if a person has an official title such as "Mayor" or "Director," always address them with their title in front of their last name rather than using Mr. or Mrs. So if you meet a mayor with the surname Wang, then address him as Mayor Wang, and not Mr. Wang. It is even more important if you happen to meet someone whose last name is Wang and is a "Deputy Mayor" or "Deputy Director" that you do NOT address him as "Deputy Mayor" or "Deputy Director," even if his name card says so or if he was so introduced. Address him instead as "Mayor Wang" or "Director Wang" or he will feel you are demeaning his status by emphasizing that his position is not the highest. If you overlook this and use American informality, you will likely ruin the relationship and doom any possible business deal.

After you get to know Chinese people a little better, say after the second or third time you meet, you should no longer use their full names to address them. If you continue to do so as you develop a relationship, they will find it a bit stiff and off-putting. Adopt instead the Chinese custom of putting the word "Lǎo" (Old) in front of their surname if they are even a day older than you, or putting "Xiǎo" (Little) in front of their surname if they are even a day younger than you. This is a term of endearment that is a perfectly acceptable form of address. For example, if a Chinese friend's last name is Lǐ and he or she is older than you, begin to call him or her "Lǎo Lǐ" as you continue to meet. It does not matter if "Lǎo Lǐ" is only twenty-five years old. As long as he or she is older than you, it is perfectly appropriate, since it's just the Chinese way of showing affection in a relationship. And if a friend has the last name Chén and is younger than you, then you should start to address him or her as "Xiǎo Chén" as your friendship develops.

In a more formal setting such as in the business world, you'll want to address Chinese people as Mr. or Ms. from the first time you meet them, just as we would in Western countries. These days in the bigger cities, shaking hands is an acceptable and common practice when people greet one another. Be warned: don't always expect to receive (or give) the "hey-how-are-ya-good-ta-see-ya" good ol' boy handshake that we Americans are so familiar with. Oftentimes handshakes are photo opportunities: looks are sometimes better than substance. In any case, at first meeting handshakes are pretty perfunctory. However, if during your time spent with the Chinese person you have established some rapport, when giving a parting handshake your new Chinese acquaintance might shake your hand warmly while putting his other hand on yours to show that he likes and trusts you. He might even put his left hand on your left arm, which will tell you that your meeting has evolved into a real friendship from his point of view. If you are meeting a woman, however, note that it is not as commonplace to shake hands. Wait until she extends her hand first. If the Chinese person does not extend his or her hand, don't miss a beat and don't interpret it as rudeness.

Just simply nod or bow slightly from the shoulders. Even when you come to know Chinese very well and establish a friendship, this is not a society where people generally hug and kiss friends. It is polite to make a slight gesture to yield the right of way to the Chinese you're getting to know at doorways, getting in cars, etc. If you are invited to visit, say, a school, factory, or some other place, the students or workers often will applaud you to both welcome you and to say goodbye. The appropriate way to respond is to applaud back with a smile. Chinese performers on the stage traditionally respond to the applause of their audience by applauding back. We've always found this a lovely custom that bespeaks humility and mutual respect. We're waiting for the day when the students at our college applaud us after a particularly inspired lesson, so we can applaud back.

Business Cards

If you are planning on doing business in China, it is essential that you bring a large supply of business cards with you. If you're only there as a tourist or a student, it is still a useful tool in making friends with the Chinese. Most Chinese in almost any walk of life have a business card. This is partially because there are so many homonyms in Chinese that a Chinese person cannot be certain how a person's name is written simply by hearing it. Only by see-ing the pictographs for the person's name can they be certain how that name is written. Business cards also show a person's occupation and status in society, which is helpful in knowing with whom you are dealing. Finally the business card provides all sorts of practical information for contacting the other person. For Chinese people the business card or "míng-piàn" ("ming-pee-en") is their identity. You are no one without it.

It is preferable if your business card has English on one side and Chinese on the other. This has become the norm for Chinese people in recent years, because of the rapidly growing contact with foreigners.

Present your card after the initial introductions, handshake, and courtesy bow.

Use both hands to present and receive cards. The Chinese and all East Asians generally use both hands to give or receive anything, especially in a formal setting. To give something with one hand is considered literally "off-handed," indifferent, and rude. When presenting your name card, hand the card over in such a way that the receiver can immediately read it right-side up, instead of having to turn the card around.

Remember that business cards in East Asia are an extension of the person. Therefore treat them with the utmost respect. This is a person's "face."

Do not write on business cards or play with them. Certainly do not put them in your back pocket and then sit down. You certainly don't want to sit on their "face"! After looking at the card carefully to note the person's name and position, it is best to hold it or place it in front of you. When you do put it away, place it in your wallet or front pocket, preferably in a cardholder just for that purpose.

Eating

When doing business in China, if the Chinese company with whom you're dealing is really interested in you they will certainly invite you to a big feast together. The Chinese do not believe in transacting any serious business before they've had at least a few good meals with any prospective business partners. If it's just a question of going out to eat with Chinese friends, however, it is necessary for you to realize that the Chinese do not believe in "Dutch treat."

They believe in "Chinese treat." This means that whomever does the inviting in a circle of friends will be the one to order for the entire group and to pay the bill for everyone. Everyone understands that the next time someone else in the group will play the host and in turn pay for everyone.

When having a meal in a restaurant or anywhere else in China, you do not order or receive your own individual dish or dishes. The host orders a variety of different dishes for everyone to share. It is considered rude for someone being treated to a meal to request any particular dishes, unless asked by the host to do so. The waiter merely gives out one menu, which the host alone looks at. It is only he or she who will order. Careful not to grab the menu from the waiter's hands, or you'll end up paying

for the meal! It is usually the custom to have a Lazy Susan or, as we like to call it, the "Wheel of Fortune." To help yourself to the common dishes that are beyond your reach at the table, simply spin the "Wheel of Fortune" slowly to have it stop with the desired dish before you. Do this carefully, of course, making sure that your Chinese friends are not right in the middle of ladling out the last of the bird's nest soup! The group-oriented nature of East Asian society, as opposed to our Western individualism, is apparent in this communal way of eating.

Sample everything at the table to be polite, even if it's only a few bites. Do not be surprised if your Chinese host selects a few pieces of meat or seafood from the common dishes with his own chopsticks and places them in your bowl with his chopsticks. This seems a bit domineering as well as unhygienic to a Westerner, but it is the Chinese host's way of showing that he wants to make sure his honored guest gets to sample the choicest morsels. Refusing any food is impolite, especially when offered like this . . . even if it's fried scorpion or roast cat. The exception here is if you are a vegetarian. In that case, you should feel free to inform your hosts of this, in which case no one will force you to eat the dishes that contain meat.

If you're at a formal banquet, which every Chinese organization will find any excuse to host, pace yourself. There are often a dozen or more courses!

Try to eat with chopsticks. They very likely may be the only eating utensils available anyway. Unless, that is, you carried a fork with you in your breast pocket all the way from your home country. Even if your host should take you to a restaurant that is not up to Western standards of hygiene, it is considered insulting for you as a guest to clean your rice bowl or chopsticks with your napkin or a wet towel. This would hint to the host that you find the establishment unclean. If your Chinese business associate or friend is playing host, be sure to make some positive comments on the food. To not do so is considered rude.

Slurping noodles or soup or even your tea is acceptable. Burping is not considered rude, either. Also, be aware that making the sound "mmm" to show you find the food delicious, is not understood by the Chinese. When Larry made this sound to show his appreciation for his Chinese mother-in-law's culinary prowess, she responded, "Does that mean he likes it or hates it?" Better to simply say "delicious" or, even better, use the equivalent Chinese expression: "hǎo chī" ("how-chir").

Leave a small amount of food on your plate or in your bowl at the end of each course to show you're finished and have had enough. An empty plate or bowl is an invitation for your host to refill it.

Don't ever take the last bit of food on a serving dish, since this will show you are still hungry.

China is generally not a dessert culture, though when they

do make something sweet it is usually done with fruit or rice. The last course of a meal is usually fresh fruit. In the summer that usually means watermelon. There are also sweet desserts such as Bā Bǎo Fàn ("Eight Treasures Rice") and variations of sweet rice or bean soup.

When you're done eating, place your chopsticks on the table or on the chopstick rest, if one is provided. Never put them across the top of your bowl or, worse yet, stick them straight up in your rice. The former is just bad manners but the latter is strictly taboo because it reminds the Chinese how offerings of vertical incense sticks are traditionally made to the spirits of their dead ancestors . . . definitely bad form for the dinner table.

A few words about seating etiquette with a group of people: the host always asks the highest-ranking guests to sit next to him, at the head of the table. If the table is round, the lowest-ranking members of the group are placed furthest from the host and most important guests, namely across the table from them. The general rule is that the highest-ranking person sits furthest from the door. If there's a focal point in the room, such as a painting or potted plant, then the highest-ranking person should be seated right in front of that object.

Drinking

Drinking alcohol at business banquets is common. The greater percentage of Chinese men with whom you make friends will also probably order some alcohol with the meal. There are many brands of Chinese beer and the Chinese always order the large party-size bottles to share. Women in China usually do not drink much alcohol. If you're just out with Chinese friends, it's fine for a Western woman to enjoy some beer. But when doing business, women should generally avoid alcohol. If offered some, we suggest that Western businesswomen accept the drink, take a sip, and set it down.

At a banquet or when going out with Chinese friends, the host will offer the first toast. Though the beer may be poured for you, only start drinking *after* the toast. It is not polite to start drinking alone. After the host makes the first toast, anyone can offer a simple toast to people sitting near him or to everyone at the table. Just raising your glass and making eye contact is a sufficient toast.

If you are a woman, and do not drink alcohol, use tea, soda, or juice for the toast. If you are a man and do not drink alcohol, it is a little harder for the Chinese to accept your toasting with a non-alcoholic beverage, since this might appear to them as insincere. If your principles or the condition of your health really do not permit you to drink any alcohol whatsoever, try to explain why you are drinking tea or juice instead. Not drinking any beverage when a toast is offered would be considered rude.

When being treated to a meal, it is impolite for you as the guest to ask for any alcoholic beverage. The host will, however, usually invite you to drink beer or hard liquor, in which case you can certainly accept. In fact, when doing business with people from smaller companies in the north of China, if you are close to reaching an agreement your Chinese partners will expect you to drink copious amounts of whiskey with them, to cement your friendship. If your constitution can stand it, it really would be best to acquiesce.

It is the duty of the host and people seated near the host—but not the wait staff—to keep refilling everyone else's glasses. If you only want to drink a little beer, be careful to not drain your glass, or else you'll very quickly find that your host or his neighbor has filled it back up for you.

Unlike in American restaurants, tea is not served with the meal unless you request it. It is often served at the end of the meal. If you don't wish a refill, leave your cup rather full to show that you do not want any more.

Smoking

More than 60% of Chinese men smoke, compared to only 23% of American men. Therefore it is very common for a Chinese host to offer a cigarette to his male guests. If you smoke, then it would be best to accept. Next time you feel like lighting up, you should be the one to take out cigarettes, if you have them, and offer them to those around you before you start smoking. For anyone to begin smoking without offering a smoke to those around you is seen as very self-centered and rude. If you aren't a smoker, you can always politely say you don't smoke, which will not offend your host. However, it would be considered very rude to ask your host or any of the other guests to not smoke. Only around 3% of Chinese women smoke, compared to around 22%

for American women. So it is unlikely that a Chinese host will offer cigarettes to a woman.

Conversation

When conversing with your new Chinese friends or business associates, try to keep the following things in mind:

You don't have to keep up a steady patter of conversation all the time. Asians are much more comfortable than Westerners with moments of silence. Remaining silent when you don't have anything important to say shows both politeness and contemplation.

Try to not talk too much about yourself. People from Western countries are all too anxious to tell someone else all about themselves. This seems very self-centered and rude to the Chinese and other Asians. Especially avoid boasting of your accomplishments or bragging about your family members. In Asian society your family members are an extension of yourself. Boasting about them is the same as boasting about oneself. Try to talk instead about matters of common interest.

There are certain things that are considered rude to ask someone in Western countries but are perfectly acceptable in China. For example, it is not considered impolite to ask someone their age or how much money they make.

It is best to not discuss politics, even if your Chinese friend or business associate brings up the topic. Subjects to avoid include the current leadership, Taiwan, Tibet, and military issues.

Good conversation topics would include the recent modernization of China and its amazing economic growth, the fast pace of change, and the current reforms. Though your knowledge of this may be limited, simply expressing awe and admiration for China today will usually be met with enthusiasm. The Chinese also usually enjoy discussing the differences between China and the West.

Do not be surprised if your Chinese friend or business associate should hesitate when questioned about his or her opinion concerning other issues. China has been a Communist society for many decades now. The Chinese are used to being told what to think by the Communist Party. They have not been encouraged in school or in the workplace to form their own opinions about anything. It is very common to hear a number of people all express an identical opinion independent of one another. For example, these days if you ask the "man on the street" what he thinks of Chairman Mao and the legacy he left behind, do not be surprised if everyone says the same thing: 70% good, 30% bad. After you've asked various Chinese this same question and received exactly the same answer, it finally dawns on you that they're all parroting the government line. Several decades earlier had you asked the same question about Chairman Mao, the general answer would have been: "Just like the First Emperor, Mao ruled with an iron hand but was therefore able to accomplish big things."

Gift Giving

In any culture gift giving helps cement friendships. When making friends in China it is always nice to give your new friend some small present. The gift need not be anything expensive. It's the idea that counts. Preferably you should give something from your home country. Young people would love to receive CDs of popular music or T-shirts, especially ones with English on them. For older people, high-quality pens or picture books of your home state or country make nice gifts. When doing business in China, be aware that officially, gifts are forbidden because of concerns over corruption. Small token gifts, however, are acceptable. It is important that these gifts do not appear to be bribes. Give the top-ranking Chinese associate or client a slightly better gift than the slightly lower-ranking executives with whom you come in contact. Those executives should be given equal gifts of slightly lesser value. After getting to know Chinese people well, it is always a nice gesture to give them a present for their children. It is harder to give an appropriate present to a middle-aged man, for instance, but he will be delighted that you were so thoughtful as to consider his child. With the one-child policy in the cities, their child will most likely be the apple of their eye.

Whether giving presents to a new friend or a business associate, gift items given in multiples of two are representative of good luck and happiness. The number four, however, is unlucky in China, since the word for four and the word for death are homonyms. When giving a present to a new friend, it is not necessary

to wrap the present. In a business setting, however, it is best to wrap the present simply or in an attractive box. Do not use white wrapping paper, since white is symbolic of funerals. Taboo gifts include clocks, since the Chinese word for clock, "zhong" ("jung") sounds exactly like the word for "the end." Do not give umbrellas, since the word for umbrella is a homonym for the word that means "separation" or "breaking up." Of course, never give as a present any company items, i.e., swag, with the company's logo on it, even if it was expensive and you had to pay for the item yourself. It will appear you are giving your Chinese friend or associate something you received for free.

If you present a card along with a present, be sure not to write on it with red ink. Red ink is often used when writing a "Dear John" or "Dear Mary" letter to end a relationship. Gifts should be given in private to save embarrassment or jealousy. Offer and receive gifts with both hands. As previously mentioned, it is rude to give or receive almost anything with just one hand, since it literally appears to be "off-handed." It is the custom for the recipient to refuse a gift several times before accepting it, though this is often very subtle and tactfully done. Do not give up just because your friend or associate seems to be reluctant to receive the present. When invited to someone's home to visit always bring a gift. Appropriate gifts might include any food items such as fruit or sweets, useful items for the whole family like hand towels with pretty or amusing designs on them or some small gadget, as well as toys or games for any children the family might have. Don't be surprised or disappointed if your friends or associates don't open the present you give them. Gifts are seldom opened in front of the giver. That custom is to save face for the giver should the recipient show any disappointment on opening his or her present. Besides, should the receiver hastily rip open the package to see what it is, that would smack of greediness. With long-term acquaintances and friends, however, you can urge them to open the present right away.

We should note that when entering a Chinese person's apartment, you should always offer to take off your shoes. If your host offers you some tea or coffee, always sip at least a little to be polite, even if you don't usually drink those beverages.

Dress

China is not a culture where people dress very formally. For daily work life "business casual" is the norm. If you're doing business in China, however, for negotiations as well as scheduled business meetings, formal business attire is expected. For a business meeting, men should either wear a formal suit and tie, or, just as in the West, they can simply wear a dress shirt and tie. But in the south of China, since it's hot and the humidity is high, and not every building has air-conditioning, for young and middle-aged businessmen to wear nice, formal short-

sleeved shirts is acceptable. This is not true for older businessmen, however, who are expected to wear a formal suit and tie.
All colors should be a darker and conservative color, such as
dark blue or gray or black, except for a white shirt, of course.
Flashy colors are frowned upon.

When women attend a business meeting, a pantsuit, or a formal blouse with skirt are acceptable. For the most part, dresses
are not considered business attire. For younger businesswomen
a formal blouse and dress slacks are considered acceptable.

Chinese businesswomen do not wear a lot of jewelry when
attending a meeting. They might just wear a pair of earrings,
but no large, showy pieces, and costume jewelry is avoided.
Chinese people do not believe in showing individuality and expressing their personality with unique or ostentatious jewelry.
For men to wear an earring or a necklace would be considered
very strange, indeed, and we would advise anyone doing business or anything official to avoid such adornments. In China,
the emphasis is on not being conspicuous or standing out from
the crowd.

Middle-aged and older Chinese businesswomen almost never wear any makeup. Young businesswomen are told to wear as
little makeup as possible. It's not that makeup is taboo, as it was
three decades ago in China. But to use a lot of makeup would
show a greater concern for personal appearance than for the
business at hand. It's not so important to look glamorous as it is
to look like you are serious about doing business, which is why
red nail polish is never used by Chinese businesswomen.

There is no restaurant in China where men are expected to wear a coat and tie in order to be allowed in. But the better discos and nightclubs will not allow you to enter if you're wearing a T-shirt, shorts, or tennis shoes. For the disco or club scene you'll need to wear better casual clothes, with slacks for men or women and dress shoes.

For street wear, except for very short shorts and miniskirts, almost anything is fine in China today. In the largest cities, these days you will see shorts are very much accepted for the male population, from young boys to very old men. However, generally only younger women in their teens to early thirties will wear shorts in public. You will almost never see a middle-aged or older woman in shorts on the street. Nevertheless, most places in China will be extremely hot in the summer. For Western tourists who are only sightseeing, no matter what your age or gender, feel free to wear shorts in order to be more comfortable. The Chinese expect us Westerners to be different, and we're going to stick out anyway.

Chinese are used to foreigners, and in particular Americans, wearing more informal clothing than they themselves would find desirable, including T-shirts or shorts. However, it is frowned upon for women in particular to show too much skin by

 sporting low necklines or baring their arms or backs. Nose rings or tongue rings are considered extremely weird, and tattoos are not looked on favorably. China is not a puritanical culture, however. It's not like many conservative Islamic countries, so any violation of standard dress or appearance is not going to offend anyone. It's just a question of presenting oneself in the best light.

On the other hand, whenever you have any kind of meeting arranged with the Chinese, whether formal or informal, whether for business or pleasure, it would be much more respectful for men to wear long pants and women to wear either slacks, a dress, or a skirt. As for formal parties, for women pantsuits, dresses, and formal gowns are all fine. But once again, it is not deemed appropriate to show too much skin. For parties, however, you can certainly sport more jewelry than in a business meeting. The Chinese like to wear the real thing rather than costume jewelry. Clothing standards, as in the U.S., are much easier for men. A nice dress shirt and slacks are all that are expected.

In the West, it is considered fine for women to wear high-heel fancy sandals that lack any strap. Chinese women would be loathe to wear any footwear like that, because it shows too much of the foot. The style also reminds the Chinese of flip-flops, which are cheap. Chinese women usually put on nylon stockings when wearing a skirt and sandals, even on the hottest days. Many women will wear ankle-length nylons even when wearing slacks and sandals, in order to avoid showing any skin. You don't have to follow suit, but you should be aware that this is the fashion.

What might be surprising to a foreigner in China is not only that Chinese women tend to dress more conservatively than American women, but that a Chinese woman might wear a nicely cut blouse that is almost completely transparent. There is no tank top underneath and so the bra is very visible. In China this is not considered inappropriate or strange, whereas it would be in the West.

Chinese people, and in fact all East Asians, are brand-crazy. They put great stock in wearing fancy brand-name clothing, if they can afford it.

The main thing for Americans to realize is how Americans tend to be the least formal in dress of all cultures in the developed world, and even in developing nations, like China, people in the large cities tend to dress in more formal clothing than do Americans.

Language

It would be best if you could learn a few basic phrases in Chinese before visiting China. If you have no previous knowledge of Chinese, refer to our chapter on speaking Chinese that you will find later in this book. We provide you with basic phrases that you will find very useful. Using them will also help you show that you are making some small effort to speak their language and thereby are showing a measure of respect for the culture you have entered. Since we assume that the majority of our readers do not speak Chinese, when speaking English with Chinese people remember to speak slowly and clearly.

If your Chinese friend or associate does not understand you, it really does not help to speak louder. Just speak more slowly and clearly. Allow some pauses in your speech to make sure the other person is following the gist of what you're saying.

If you're speaking on the phone, be patient with what sounds like silence. If the Chinese person is speaking in English, it is very possible he or she is trying to think of how best to express an idea in your language, which is foreign to them.

Physical Contact and Gestures

Every culture has its own sense of personal space. Americans in particular find the Chinese comfort zone regarding distance a bit too close for their liking. Try to accept that when Chinese converse with you, they might step closer to you than is customary in the West. On the other hand, the Chinese do not like to be touched, especially by strangers. So don't hug, backslap, or put your hand on their arm. You will see people of the same sex walking hand in hand on the street, but that is only for close friends. Finally, never point to someone with your index finger, as Westerners do. Rather use your open hand to gesture in their direction.

15

Restaurants

One of the biggest joys in coming to China is sampling what is arguably the world's greatest cuisine. Chinese cooking offers a far greater variety of outstanding dishes than any other culture in the world. "Chinese food" at restaurants in China bears only minimal resemblance to the "Chinese food" you may have encountered in the U.S. For the most part only restaurants in southern China will have Cantonese-style dishes like sweet and sour pork or moo-goo gai-pan. Beijing duck can only really be enjoyed in Beijing. And if, like Larry, you're fond of "ru-shan," fan-shaped fried pieces of goat cheese, then you'll find it only in certain areas of Yunnan Province in the southwest. Every region of China has many of its own specialty dishes, most of which are not found on any Chinese-American restaurant menus. And no restaurant in China offers egg rolls or crab Rangoon or even fortune cookies, which are a Western invention.

In China you'll also never find dishes like "Amazing Chicken" or "Shrimp with Assorted Vegetables" or "General Tso's Chicken." Things like "Chop Suey" belong to another era entirely, a time when Chinese chefs in America were catering to American tastes. After all, Americans generally like anything

that's fried. We also like anything that's sweet. Put them together, as in "General Tso's Chicken," and you have a definite winner. Many of the things we order in a Chinese-American restaurant, such as "Happy Family" or "Three Delicacies," also reflect the approach to cooking invented by Chinese-American chefs. That is to say, throw a whole bunch of vegetables together with one kind of meat or seafood, add some tasty sauce, and you have a complete meal in one dish. It's the American preference for one-stop shopping.

Real Chinese food rarely combines more than one type of meat or seafood with one type of vegetable. Often there is just one meat or one vegetable stir-fried separately in one of hundreds of types of sauces. That's because Chinese people generally order at least five or six different dishes for every meal in a restaurant. When Americans go out to eat in a restaurant, each person generally orders his or her own single dish of food. On the other hand, when Chinese people eat out in a restaurant, many dishes are ordered for the whole group to enjoy together. Thus, there is no reason to throw every ingredient into one all-purpose dish "chop suey" style. Because the prices for food in China are so much less than in countries like the U.S., you can afford to order at least five or six different dishes for even just two people and still only end up paying ten U.S. dollars per person.

A big mistake many foreigners make is to limit their dining choices to what is found in their hotel. While this may be a "safe" choice, most hotel restaurants are overpriced and only mediocre in their menu offerings. An increasing number of restaurants in most major cities in China offer English menus, and new street-savvy guidebooks are moving beyond listing only hotel choices, as was the case when venturing out was only for the adventurous. Since restaurants can appear quickly and disappear equally quickly in the new, free-enterprise China, check with your hotel staff to make sure that any restaurant you read about in the guidebooks is still in business. The hotel staff are often too young and have too thin a wallet to know enough to give advice about the best restaurants in town. But sometimes there is a concierge who can recommend the best place to go for dinner outside of the hotel.

A word of advice about reading a menu in a Chinese restaurant: When a dish has an exotic sounding name, find out whether the name is being used poetically or literally. "Braised lion heads" are really delicious pork meatballs in a delightful, mildly piquant sauce that you will not want to miss. Similarly "ants climbing the tree" is really a famous if rather simple spicy dish comprised of "cellophane" noodles (made from green beans) and bits of ground pork that look a bit like ants.

On the other hand, some dishes have exotic names you must take literally. "Fēngzǐ" or "bee babies" are really roasted bee

larvae. They're as yummy as roasted soybeans, but you should realize that the title of the dish, in this case, is exactly what they are. "Niúbiān," literally, "cow braid," is in fact stewed bull penis. When the restaurant lists "lips of deer " or "monkey brain" you need to take them at their word. "Zhújié chóng," or "bamboo worms" are maggots that look like jointed bamboo. When stir-fried in oil to a golden brown, they're as tasty as French fries. But in order to know what you'll be getting, do ask your waitperson whether you should read the name of the dish literally or figuratively. In the province of Guangdong in the south you really have to be careful. An old adage goes that diners there will eat anything with four legs except a table and anything that flies except an airplane!

There is another curve ball the Chinese will throw a foreign tourist in restaurants. Just because the menu may feature descriptions in English doesn't always mean they will be intelligible. This phenomenon, which can be encountered almost anywhere in China, is a peculiar takeoff on English that many simply call "Chinglish," but which we prefer to call "English Made in China," or "E.M.C." To help you decipher a typical menu in a restaurant in China, we present some excerpts from a menu in the popular tourist town of Lijiang in southwestern China. The restaurant in question is a lovely place situated along a creek in the heart of this eight-hundred-year-old village in the mountains. In the 1990s it was declared a UNESCO World Heritage Site and is now inundated with visitors from all over the world as well as from all over China.

The samples from the menu (below) will give you some idea of how to make sense of and interpret other "E.M.C." menus to be found all over the country.

English version of the Jiannanchun Restaurant menu in Lijiang:

Bin curd → "bean curd," i.e., "tofu"

Ham bowel → "pig intestines"

Fish Soup with Pungent and Tingling Flavor
   → hot and spicy fish in a hot pot

Braided hare → braised hare

Dill picks Fish → dill-pickled fish

Fried chicken and Chinese Chest Nuts

Bouilli → i.e., "red-cooked pork"

Fried Rabbit Meat with Wild Prickle → fried rabbit
   with wild mountain peppers

Wild Prickle Made Chicken Paws → wild mountain
   peppers with chicken feet

Couple Lung Pieces → i.e., "Husband and wife pork
   lung slices"

Rabbit Cubes with Chilly Oil → "cooked in oil flavored with hot chili peppers"

Tasty Cooked Peanut → i.e., fried peanuts

A Class Yun cigaret → a class "A" cigarette from Yunnan Province

Melon Pork Chip Soup → i.e., soup with winter melon and pork slices

Purely Stewed Beef Soup → soup with stewed beef ribs cooked without soy sauce

Deep Fried Bee Cocoons

Stewed Chicken with Chinese Caterpillar Fungus

Deep Fried Dragonflies

While there's nothing particularly funny about the last three dishes, these are examples of dishes you must take literally. One thing that you may find "funny" in a different sense is that in less expensive restaurants, you will discover that an additional charge of 1 yuan per person has been added to the bill for the wet towel they automatically give you as well as an extra yuan per person for your rice bowl and chopsticks, which have been "sterilized" and encased in plastic wrap!

The dishes you'll find in most restaurants in China will not include anything as exotic as deep-fried bees or dragonflies. You will find, however, an absolutely amazing variety of delicious selections. There will be countless meat and seafood dishes you have never heard of before and many kinds of vegetables you can't find in a restaurant in the U.S. or other Western countries, from leafy green vegetables like "kōngxīncài" and "xiàncài" to lotus root. Vegetarians should look for dishes with the suffix "cài" (菜), which means "vegetables."

If you're not a vegetarian, don't leave Beijing without trying the city's signature dish, Beijing duck! Also sample the favorite food of the Chinese, "jiǎozi" (饺子). These are the Chinese ravioli. The standard filling was once minced pork, Chinese cabbage, and ginger, but these tasty delights are now offered with every kind of combination of meats, seafood, and vegetables imaginable. Three of our favorites include those stuffed with pork and fennel, medley of wild mushrooms, and tomato and egg. Dip them in a mixture that's part soy sauce and part vinegar and it's easy to make a full meal of these scrumptious dumplings.

Our main advice regarding food in China is to be adventurous. As long as you're dining in a fairly decent and clean-looking restaurant, dare to try some dishes that you've never had before but that seem appealing. More and more restaurants have English translations of their offerings, so you'll have some idea what you're getting. Don't be like one of our students, who spent the entire three months of our college's semester program in Beijing eating nothing but sweet and sour pork for every meal! From the country with arguably the world's greatest and most varied cuisine, it is a crime to return home without having sampled at least some of its extraordinary culinary delights.

16 English Made in China

In the previous chapter we introduced the concept of "E.M.C.," or "English Made in China." With millions of foreign tourists coming to China each year, China is putting up considerably more signs in English as well as Chinese. This all seems very reassuring until you soon realize that the English they're using is not the English you've been taught. It's not the King's or Queen's English, either. In fact, it's quite unlike any English known to man or woman. Playing on the famous slogan, you could refer to it as "English with Chinese Characteristics."

The sample restaurant menu in the previous chapter is just one example of encountering "E.M.C." There are signs in airports, in parks, in museums, on packages of snack food, all of which employ this Chinese version of English. Here are some examples:

Airports

Sign in Beijing Airport:
No entry in peacetime (i.e., Emergency Exit only)

Kunming Airport Security sign:
No controlled dirks;

No in Flam Mables
No Truncheons

Sign in Xian Airport over a store that is the only authorized
seller of certain goods:
Monopoly Shop

Trains
Sign on train washroom between Beijing and Tianjin:
No occupying while stabling (i.e., don't use when train is in the
station)

Cablecars
Sign by the cablecar in Kunming for the International Horticul-
tural Gardens:
Armymen teachers and retiring people rely on credentials con-
cerned can have 5 yuan preferential treatment. The oldmen over
70 yrs. old people of heart diease, hypertension deformity and fear-
ing high politely refuse to take cable car. (faithfully reprinted
complete with original typos)

Taxicabs
Notice in back seat of taxi in Kunming, with picture of a fox,
asking if you know which animal it is:
The policemen remind you:
Please remember the animal's name and code. Please don't leave
anything in the car.

Hotels

Guest information booklet for the Bell Tower Hotel in Xian:

> The recreation and fitness department lies in the 2nd floor, offer sauna massage in 24 hrs. to you, cosmetology, idle amusement service, that chess and card, etc. are repaired, luxurious environment, hospitable service, awaits your presence.
>
> The great kindness and support of the recreation and fitness dept. specially pursue the favorable activity for guests in order to thank for guests long-term, the service is not reduced, it is more to be favorable. Welcome your presence again.

Sign for massage in four-star hotel:

> Massage:
> Pull out the fire bottle
> Medicine the wash foot
> Degeneration of the parts of the vertebrae

Card in a room in the Bell Tower Hotel, Xian, warning against outside "massage" services:

> In order to ensure your safety of human life and property, if receive the message (meaning "massage") service telephone that the hotel external world offers, please refuse.

Restaurants

Sign in Xian teahouse:

> melon seeds, peanuts, nosh 3 yuan plate (note: "nosh" is the Yiddish word for "snack")

Paper cover for dispos-
able chopsticks:

> *For your health Please
> use sanitanen chop-
> sticks (i.e., sanitized
> chopsticks)*

Packaged Food Items

In a gift shop in the Xian Airport on a box of chocolates in the
shape of the terra-cotta warriors in the First Emperor's tomb:

> *Qin Terra-Cotta is one biggest buring mount of the Qin Shi Huang
> Mausoleum. It is composed by Chariots, Cavalryman, Infantry-
> man, Including the General officer.*
>
> *All these Terra-Cotta have different facial expression,
> various dressing.*
>
> *They were arranged in the military formation which pro-
> vides the best material for the study of Qin Dynasty's army.
> Our chocolate is the copy of the Terra-Cotta army.*

On a package of cookies given on domestic flights in China:

> *Increase into the real object material of original flavor, through
> dispensing of*
>
> > *Science, in really ideal good product that enjoy of delicacy.*

Parks and Gardens

Sign at entrance to Heilongtan Park in Lijiang, Yunnan Province:

> *Which to below 1.3 m child, holding the disabled card, holding the retired card personnel and 70 yr. old of above old person should give free of them, to the serviceman, the student which has the corresponding credential should give the half-price preferential treatment.*

Sign in the Hanshan Temple of Suzhou:

> *Conscientiously maintain public hygiene.*
> *No spitting, pissing, shitting, or littering at wrong places.*
> *No fight, gambling, or hooliganism.*

Sign in national park of Jiuzhaigou:

> *Retiring area* (i.e., rest area for tourists)

Tourist brochure for Jiuzhaigou National Park:

> *Next to Jiuzhaigou Valley and Huanglong, the counties of Maoxian and Wenchuan are the place where the Zang and Qiang nationality live together. The wood-board houses and barbicans are distributed in the green mountain and waters. The local people are homeliness and soulful and hospitality to guests. If you are agreed, you may be a guest of their family. You must get candies ready for the children, and you may be welcome. Buttered tea is one of the main foods. June 6 of the lunar calendar every year is the Temple Fair Day of Huanglong Temple, when thousands of people from all*

directions gather here,
having a jolly time.

Museums and
Historic Sites

Sign on Xian History Museum:
> *Temporary exhibitions which offer freshness to the viewers.*

Captions by art work in the Xian History Museum:
> *A making up concubine* (Ming painting of a courtesan apply-
> ing makeup)
> *Pottery figure of an unfree peasant* (figurine of a farmer)

Theaters

Pamphlet for audience in theater in Xian:
> *This show translates the marrow of the traditional culture with
> modern arctic ideal and showing method. The theater with the
> ultra open consciousness, the modern bearing and the compatabil-
> ity with the world which became meny-faceted, face to the head of
> state, official business, tour and social contact, technical commu-
> nication, leisure and entertainment etc. all kinds of consumers.*

Pearl of the Orient Tower in Shanghai:
> *The ragamuffin, drunken people and psychotics are forbidden to
> enter the Tower.*

No smoking at non-appointed spot.

Prohibit carrying tinder and explosive (banger, match, lighter), restricted cutter (kitchen knife, scissors, fruit knife, sword, and so on), and metal-made electric appliance.

Prohibit carrying the animals and articles which disturb the common sanitation (including the peculiar smell of effluvium).

Prohibit carrying the articles which can destroy and pollute inner environment of the Tower.

Prohibit carrying dangerous germs, pests, and other baleful biology. Forbid any articles from epidemic areas.

Prohibit hanging streamer, slogan, and any other prints in the Tower, including commerce, politics, religion and so on.

The cubage of liquid article which the tourist carries can't overage one milliliter and must accept examination. . . .

Learning Chinese

Despite China's rich history and civilization, the Chinese language is not that difficult to learn. For one thing, there are no difficult rules of conjugation to master as in Western languages. Instead of saying "I see, you see, he/she sees" the Chinese say "Wǒ kàn, nǐ kàn, tā kàn." The word "Tā" (he or she) denotes both masculine and feminine in spoken Chinese.

Because there is no conjugation, there is no use of tense in Chinese either. Instead of saying, "I saw her yesterday" the Chinese simply say, "I yesterday see she." Since we're talking about yesterday, it is what we call "past tense." There is no declension. Instead of saying, "I see her; she sees me" the Chinese simply say the equivalent of "I see she; she see I."

Chinese is a tonal language. That means that you must make your voice go up or down to change the meaning of a word. Mandarin Chinese, the dialect that has been the "national language" for many centuries, fortunately only has four different tones. Each word you learn will use one of those tones. Count your blessings. Had Cantonese been chosen as the national language, you would have had to learn six tones. Four tones are enough to handle, thank you very much.

Fortunately, we have the same four tones or intonations in English. The difference is that how we intone a word in English doesn't completely change the definition of the word, only the feeling behind it. Consider the sound "oh" for example. If we say the word "oh" with a high, level pitch, sustaining it for a second or two, as in "ooohhh, that's great!" we have the "first tone" in Chinese. This can be indicated by a tone mark, which is a line running over the vowel of the word to indicate its tone, or by a number in parentheses immediately following the word:

First tone: ˉ high level tone
Second tone: ´ rising tone
Third tone: ˇ downward before rising up
Fourth tone: ` sharp downward tone

If we say the same sound "oh" with a rising intonation, as if we're asking the question "oh, is that so?" then we have the second tone in Mandarin Chinese. If we offer sympathy to someone by saying "oh" with a falling intonation but with our voice rising back up at the end, as in "oh, that's too bad," we have the third tone in Chinese. Finally if we say "oh" with our voice starting fairly high up and falling, as in "oh, that's cool," we have the fourth and final tone of Chinese. Make sure that when you learn a word in Chinese you learn the correct tone, or you could be in big trouble. Unlike in English, when you change the tone of a word in Chinese, it completely changes the dictionary definition of a word as well as the "character" or "pictograph" with which it's written.

Here are some examples of the difference a tone can make to a word.

Let's take the famous example of the sound "ma." Now in almost every language of the world "ma" means "mother." It does in Chinese, too, but only if you pronounce "ma" with the first tone. If you say "ma" with the second or "rising" tone, it means "marijuana!" If you say it with the third tone, "ma" means "horse." Now, you don't want to go calling your mother a horse, do you? If you say "ma" with the fourth or "falling" tone, then you've changed the meaning once again, this time to "curse; scold; yell at."

Here is a full Chinese sentence. See if you can figure out what it means. We'll indicate which tone you need to use. For example: "mā mà mǎ." So what does that mean? Of course, any Chinese person can tell you that "Mom yelled at the horse." Now, we don't know exactly what the horse did to make Mom so mad, but it must have been something pretty bad. We suggest you don't try the same shenanigans as that horse!

Here's another example of the importance of saying the tones correctly. A young American is studying elementary Chinese with a lovely young Chinese woman. He says: "Wo yao wen

ni" (I want to ask you), but he's not sure of the tone for the word "wen," which means "to ask." So he tries the second tone and says: "Wó yào wén nǐ." Unfortunately, "wen" with the second tone, means "to smell." Oops. The young woman shakes her head. The young man realizes that he's said the tone wrong and tries another tone instead. This time he says emphatically: "Wó yào wěn nǐ" (I want to kiss you). "Wen" with the third tone means to kiss. The young woman is about to leave the room. Finally in desperation the young man shouts out: "Wǒ yào wèn nǐ." Ah, the fourth tone did it. "What do you want to ask me?" the young woman finally replies, much relieved.

We offer below a short list of the top twenty phrases we suggest you learn for your time in China. Learning these won't make you able to discuss in Chinese the re-valuation of the Chinese yuan vis-à-vis the American dollar. But they will help you get your basic needs met. Pay particular attention to the tones of the words! By trying to speak at least a few words in Chinese, you're showing some respect for the Chinese culture by caring enough to have learned at least a little of the language.

There are also no plurals in Chinese. Instead of saying "one mouse; two mice" or "one house; two houses" the Chinese just say the equivalent of "one mouse; two mouse" or "one house; two house." Blessedly there is no noun gender in Chinese, written or spoken. This is a relief after studying languages such as Spanish or French, where you have to figure out whether a table, for instance, is masculine or feminine, depending presumably on how shapely the legs are.

If Chinese is so simple, then why don't all Americans pick it up as fast as they learn to use a cell phone? One factor is the fact that there are almost no cognates between Chinese and English. That is to say that there are very few words in Chinese that sound like their equivalent in English. Around 60% of words in French or Spanish have words that sound somewhat similar to the word with the same meaning in English. That's because of our common Latin roots.

In Chinese, a hamburger is a "hànbǎobāo" ("hahn-bow-bow, with the "bow" pronounced as in "to bow before a king"). Coca-Cola is "kěkǒukělè" ("kuh-koh-kuh-luh" = "pleases mouth, can have joy"). And a computer is, of course, "diàn-nǎo" ("dien-now"), literally "electric brain." In other words, if you want to learn some Chinese, you'll have to forget about getting any help from English or French or German. You'll need to learn to make some strange sounds that will be totally unfamiliar to you.

One of the particular joys of speaking Chinese with Chinese people is their delight that a foreigner can say anything at all in their language beyond "nǐ hǎo" ("knee how"), meaning "hello." As a foreign tourist in Paris or Berlin you have to speak French or German very well indeed to impress the natives, but in China you get big strokes as a foreigner for being able to say just a few phrases in Chinese. Chinese is so different from Western languages that few Western tourists ever bother to learn even one word of it.

Below are our top Chinese phrases. We first give the standard transliteration in *pinyin*, followed by our own transliteration in normal type to help you with the pronunciation. Note there are some instances that when the same character is repeated twice, the tone of the second character is dropped.

Hello → *nǐ hǎo* → knee how.
(Think: How's your knee, i.e., "How are you?")

Goodbye → *zàijiàn* → dzeye gee-en

Thank you → *xiè xie* → syeh syeh
(The second "xie" has no tone.)

You're welcome → *bú kè qi* → boo kuh chee
(The "chee" has no tone.)

Good morning → *zǎoshang hǎo* → dzow shahng how

Please stand in line → *qǐng páiduì* → ching pie dway

Too expensive → *taì guì le* → tie gway luh

(Make it) cheaper → *piányi yìdiǎn* → pien yee ee dien

(I; we) don't want it → *búyào* → boo yow

I want this one → *wǒ yào zhèige* → waw yow jay guh
(Note: "guh" has no tone)

How much (does it cost)? → *duóshǎo*

→ qian dwo shao chee-en

Where is the bathroom? → *cèsuǒ zài nǎlǐ*
→ tsuh swo dz-eye nah lee

Over there → *nàli* → nah lee
(Note: "lee" has no tone)

Please give me → *qǐng gěi wǒ* → ching gay waw

Fine; OK; good; alright → *hǎo* → how

Not OK; no good → *bùhǎo* → boo how

I want to go ___ → *Wǒ yào qù* → waw yow chee-you
(Show taxi driver the address in Chinese.)

(Want) to go to ___ → *Wǒ yào dào* ___ *qù*
→ waw you dow ___ chee-you
(e.g., when buying tickets at train or bus station)

Police! → *jǐngchá!* → jing chah!
(in case of theft or emergency)

Help! Help! → *jiùmìng! jiùmìng!* → jee-oh ming! jee-oh ming!

Faster! → *kuài yìdiǎn!* → kweye ee dien!

Numbers one through ten:

one → *yī* → ee

two → *èr* → ar

three → *sān* → sahn

four → *sì* → szih

five → *wǔ* → woo

six → *liù* → leo

seven → *qī* → chee

eight → *bā* → bah

nine → *jiǔ* → geo

ten → *shí* → sure

one of something → *yíge* → ee guh

two of something → *liǎngge* → lee-ang guh

three of something → *sānge* → sahn guh

Etc.

One of the first things you'll notice when you arrive in China is that everywhere you look there are signs in some kind of hieroglyphic writing that looks very much like chicken tracks. Your first hunch is that some practical joker has replaced all the English or some other reasonable alphabetic language with some made-up pictures. Then you remember reading that the Chinese have their own "inscrutable" written language that is said to date back some four or five thousand years.

Of course, most Americans have seen Chinese "characters" in the U.S. We see them on storefronts in our Chinatowns as well as on some Chinese restaurant menus. We see them on T-shirts, because we consider Chinese characters beautiful and fascinating and maybe a bit mysterious. There are even Chinese characters tattooed on the bodies of our NBA basketball stars. Allen

Iverson, the star of the Philadelphia 76ers, has the Chinese pictograph "zhong" ("juhng"), or "loyalty," tattooed on his neck. Marcus Camby of the Portland Trail Blazers has two Chinese

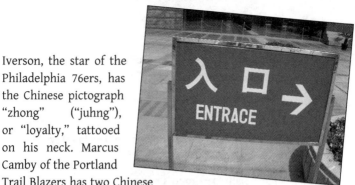

characters tattooed on one of his arms. The characters literally mean, "compelled tribe," which isn't correct Chinese. But who cares? Chinese characters are cool to most of us for the very fact that we don't understand them. It's the mystery that attracts us. And they are much prettier than any alphabet.

Actually the Chinese writing system is one of the great wonders of the world. Originally, all writing, such as hieroglyphics and cuneiform, was based on pictographs. Chinese, however, is the only non-alphabetical language that has stood the test of time and is still used today. The Japanese borrowed the Chinese writing system in the sixth century and also continue to use it.

The problem for foreign tourists, however, is that most of them don't read Chinese. They don't know whether the sign is telling them to turn right or left to go to the restroom. They don't even know if the characters they think mean "restroom" might be the characters for "pool hall" or "tanning booth."

Here are some of the most common signs you want to recognize when out and about anywhere in China.

厕所 → *cèsuǒ* ("tsuh-swoh") → **toilet**
(literally "convenience place")

卫生间 → *wèishēngjiān* ("way-shung-jee-n") → **facility**
(literally "hygiene room")

洗手间 → *xǐshǒujiān* ("see-show-jee-n") → **lavatory**
(literally "hand washing room")

男 → *nán* ("nahn") → **men's room**

女 → *nǚ* ("nee-yu") → **ladies' room**

入口 → *rù kǒu* ("ru koo") → **entrance**
(literally "entering mouth")

出口 → *chū kǒu* ("chu koo") → **exit**
(literally "leaving mouth")

售票处 → *shòupiàochù* ("show pee-ow chu") → ticket
window
(literally "selling tickets place")

出租车 → *chūzūchē* ("chu dzu chuh") → **taxicab**
(literally "out rent car ")

18

Going Home

We began by showing you what you may encounter when arriving at an airport in China. All you really need to worry about is passing immigration and navigating the airport restrooms. Getting out of China, even at the same airport at which you arrived, can be a totally different experience.

On international flights to and out of China, in economy class you are allowed two suitcases for check-in, each weighing up to 23 kilos (50 pounds), and in business or first class you are allowed two suitcases, each weighing up to 32 kilos (70 pounds).If you exceed the weight limit, you will need to pay a fine, usually at a separate ticket counter within the departure terminal, and bring the receipt of payment back to the airline representative before your luggage can be processed or put on the conveyor.

Assuming your bags are now checked through, you only need to pass through security and immigration before heading to your gate. You see there is a form you need to fill out for leaving China. It's a simple form. All you have to do is write your name, passport number, flight number, purpose of your stay in China. What the form doesn't tell you, and no person or guidebook does either, is that you must use BLUE or BLACK ink. For 99% of the flying public, that

may not be a problem. But many of us Americans these days like to use pens with red ink, or purple ink, or green ink, or even yellow ink. Larry happened to have a pen with red ink. He's a professor, after all. Many of us in the teaching trade get a thrill from marking up our students' papers and tests with red ink. So Larry, on his umpteenth time flying out of China, filled out his form in red ink in beautiful block letters.

When he reached the immigration counter and proudly presented his U.S. passport along with his beautifully hand-printed form, the officer said in gruff, barely understandable English: "No good. Led ink. Led ink." When Larry clarified in Chinese that his form was unacceptable because it was printed in red ink, Larry asked where it was written on the form or anywhere else that red ink was no good. Just policy, he was told. After twenty-five years of teaching college Chinese Larry still didn't know what every Chinese knows. Red ink is only used in China to correct mistakes. So teachers use it to grade students' homework, just like we do. It's never used for business transactions, or, apparently, for something so simple and seemingly innocuous as an immigration form.

Caught off guard and in a bit of a huff, Larry asked where he could get a blue or black pen. The immigration official pointed to a pen affixed to a nearby table. The trouble was that there was an old Chinese man filling out forms for himself and his wife, and he was filling them out with the greatest care. When Larry finally spotted another pen he could use, he traced over the red ink with the blue ink of the pen provided. He then returned to the customs counter. "No good," the man said in Chinese this time. "Led ink!" "But I traced over it . . . " "No good," Larry was told. Larry got a new form and filled it out all over again in blue ink. The information wasn't any different than the first time. But the color was right.

Larry finally caught up to his wife fifteen minutes later at the gate. After preaching to students for twenty-five years about how wonderful China was, and how they should all think of going there someday to study or to work, Larry suddenly was there at the gate shouting to his wife: "I hate this country! I'm never coming back!!" One month later, of course, he's already planning his next trip to China with some of his students. He had remembered all the reasons that had attracted him to China in the first place.

So Why Go to China?

If there are so many minor hassles to overcome in traveling to and around China, why bother to go there? Because, in spite of every small inconvenience or aggravation we've experienced in our many trips to China, for every minute we spent in anger or frustration, there were many hours or even days when we were enjoying an exciting or lovely time and didn't want to be anywhere else. That's because there is so much of value to experience in the Middle Kingdom. There is the long and richly patterned history that is preserved in its multitude of historic sites. There are the many breathtaking mountain ranges and rivers that make China one of the most scenically spectacular places on the planet. And there is without question the world's most varied and delicious cuisine.

But it is more than that, a lot more. There are the sights, smells, and sounds of a dynamic society with an energy and buzz of activity that has accompanied the new economic freedoms and prosperity. There is a sense of limitless possibilities in an era that has seen the fastest economic growth of any society in history. Then there are the people, possibly the most warm, welcoming, and good-humored of all the peoples in Asia. So many of them are amazingly brilliant, talented, and just plain wonderful. Since China has over one-fifth of the world's people, it is only natural that the country should also have over one-

fifth of the world's best and most gifted people. Finally there is the fact that, given the tremendous size of both its land and its population, coupled with its rapid economic growth, China is the emerging superpower that some day may soon rival the United States. We have a feeling that if a country is that important in the world, we all need to understand it better than we currently do.

We hope you'll visit China sometime soon. We think you'll have an extraordinary experience. Just be prepared for the many little pitfalls we've mentioned in this book and try to follow our advice, and you'll have a great time. And remember that whether you travel to China or anywhere else in the world, along with your deodorant always bring a healthy sense of humor.

Happy traveling!

Best Places to Visit in China

Top Ten Historical Sites

1. The Great Wall of China

The Great Wall of China is one of the great engineering feats of all time. It is the longest wall in the world and stretches nearly four thousand miles. As Richard Nixon proclaimed when he walked upon it, "This is a Great Wall!" Built over the centuries to protect China from barbarian invaders, it overlooks some spectacular scenery as it snakes its way across the rugged mountain terrain. Try to visit the wall at Mutianyu rather than the Badaling section that is most frequented by tourists. Mutianyu takes an hour longer to reach from Beijing, but is well worth the two-and-a-half-hour journey. Here you'll find smaller crowds, slightly easier walking, and greener and more stunning mountain scenery. Nothing says China like the Great Wall.

2. The Forbidden City in Beijing

The Forbidden City was the palace of Chinese emperors for nearly six hundred years, from the beginning of the Ming Dynasty in the fourteenth century until the overthrow of the Qing Dynasty

in 1911. Commoners were forbidden to enter the palace grounds for all those centuries, but now we're welcomed in. Located in the heart of Beijing, right across from Tiananmen Square, the complex consists of 980 buildings with nine throne rooms. There is no greater example of the grandeur of traditional China. The Palace Museum houses an extensive collection of artwork and artifacts from the imperial collections of the Ming and Qing emperors. Also be sure to stroll around the neighborhoods behind the Forbidden City.

3. The Temple of Heaven in Beijing
The complex of temples here in central Beijing was laid out in the early fifteenth century and renovated in the eighteenth and nineteenth centuries. The emperors of the Ming and Qing dynasties would come here to offer sacrifices to Heaven and pray for good harvests on behalf of the country. The beautiful buildings and 270-acre green park area make this a place worth visiting.

4. The Summer Palace near Beijing
This summer residence and playground for the imperial family in the eighteenth and nineteenth centuries covers an expanse of nearly three square kilometers, three-quarters of which

is occupied by the man-made lake in the center. The lovely grounds offer a variety of palaces, gardens, and other classical-style architectural structures. One of the most stunning sights is a long, wooden-covered walkway or corridor that is adorned with delicately painted scenes of natural beauty.

5. The Terra-Cotta Warriors of the Qin Emperor in Shaanxi Province

For the past 2,200 years a terra-cotta army has guarded the tomb of the First Emperor of China. The life-size figures of warriors and horses, dating from 210 B.C., were discovered in 1974 by some local farmers near Xian in Shaanxi Province. The figures include warriors, chariots, horses, officials, acrobats, and musicians. There are over 8,000 soldiers and 130 chariots with hundreds of clay horses discovered in the pits, placed there to protect the Qin Emperor in the afterlife. The entire tomb is larger than the Great Pyramid, but it has still not been excavated. According to Chinese historical records, magnificent treasures are buried there; these will likely be revealed to the world in the coming decades.

6. The Yungang Grottoes near Datong, Shanxi Province

The Yungang Grottoes comprise three major groups of caves with over 50,000 stone statues that were carved more than 1,500 years ago along a cliff face near the city of Datong. There are a total of 53 caves. In the largest, with a ceiling over 65 feet, stands a nearly 50-foot-high stone column shaped like a pagoda and decorated with Buddha statues and designs; 33 carved panels depict the story of the historical Buddha. Be sure also to visit the nearby "Hanging Temple" (Xuánkōngsì), a cliffside monastery built 1,500 years ago that hangs nearly 250 feet above the ground.

7. The Longmen Grottoes near Luoyang, Henan Province

The earliest of the Longmen Grottoes date from just after the Yungang Caves (see above). They were begun around 493 when the capital was moved to the city of Luoyang and continuously built during the subsequent four hundred years. There are over 1,300 caves and 100,000 statues. The largest grotto is 118 feet wide and 136 feet long. The most impressive figure here is the 56-foot-high statue of Buddha sitting cross-legged on an eight-square lotus throne. Wanfo Cave, completed in 680, has 15,000 small statues of Buddha chiseled into its walls. Behind the main stone statue of Buddha are 54 lotuses holding 54 seated Buddhist saints with various expressions.

8. The Potala Palace in Lhasa, Tibet

Now a Chinese museum, the Potala Palace was traditionally the seat of the Dalai Lama, Tibetan Buddhists' spiritual leader. Famous for its imposing white walls surrounding the inner red palace, the building sits at an altitude of 12,000 feet. The Potala Palace is located in Lhasa, the capital of the Tibetan Autonomous Region. Its setting ringed by high snow-capped mountains makes the palace all the more stunning.

9. The Ancient Walled City of Pingyao, Shanxi Province

Pingyao is the best preserved of the ancient walled towns of ancient China. It still retains its city layout from the Ming and Qing dynasties. Some four thousand residences maintain the Ming and Qing style of architecture, and the streets and storefronts appear much as they did in centuries past. The city was the financial center of China several hundred years ago. One of the ancient banks is now a museum that displays the old banking system. Part of the charm of Pingyao is the opportunity it offers to stay in inns that are renovated Qing-dynasty homes of the upper class, with lovely inner courtyards and with furnishings in the rooms that reproduce those of previous centuries.

10. The Dunhuang Caves in Gansu Province

The Mogao Caves of Dunhuang in northwest China are a UNESCO World Heritage Site filled with exquisite Buddhist art and manuscripts. According to legend, in the fourth century a monk had a vision of a thousand Buddhas above the desert at Dunhuang. This inspired the creation of these famous caves, which were carved out of the rock and filled with the manuscripts and treasures by monks seeking enlightenment in this remote place. In the vicinity stands the White Horse Pagoda, built by a monk from India to honor the horse that died on the journey from China. Visiting the nearby town as well as the remarkable sand dunes in the area will give you some idea of the ancient Silk Road that connected China with Central Asia and Rome.

The Ancient River Villages of China

The following are the best examples of ancient villages built along rivers that preserve the architecture of past centuries as well as Chinese folk history.

1. Xidi and Hongcun in Anhui Province

Located in Yixian County, Xidi and Hongcun Ancient Villages give visitors the chance to see daily life in ancient China as well as to admire priceless cultural treasures. These villages are over nine hundred years old and preserve the ancient architectural styles of that time. In the village of Xidi are 124 ancient residences. All contain intricate carvings of birds, flowers, and human figures. Hongcun Village is surrounded by green hills and has two streams, two main streets, and nearly a hundred lanes, with around 140 centuries-old homes. These villages were made famous when they were featured in the movie *Crouching Tiger, Hidden Dragon*; the stunning duel in a canopy of bamboo trees was shot in the neighboring mountains. Near the villages are the scenic Huangshan Mountains (see below). The ancient town of Huangshan is one of the lovelier and more peaceful smaller cities in China. These two villages, when combined with the Huangshan Mountains and the city of Huangshan, along with the surrounding countryside, make this one of our favorite places to visit in all of China.

2. The Villages of Zhujiajiao, Zhouzhuang, and Tongli, near Shanghai

The three villages of Zhujiajiao, Zhouzhuang, and Tongli have preserved or restored buildings that have been converted into shops, restaurants, and inns on either side of a central river with connecting canals. All make pleasant day trips from Shanghai.

3. Old Phoenix Town in Hunan Province

Old Phoenix Town is similar to the river villages of Zhujiajiao, Zhouzhuang, and Tongli, and far enough from Zhangjiajie to require an overnight stay.

Top Ten Scenic Sites

1. Guilin and Yangshuo in Guangxi Province

The strange but beautiful karst mountain formations along the Li River, between the small city of Guilin and the town of Yangshuo, are justifiably the most famous scenic attraction in China. They have inspired many centuries of Chinese landscape paintings and have appeared in many movies about China. The area is rich with scenic beauty, including some famous limestone caves and the incredibly beautiful terraced rice fields of Longji. Rather than stay in Guilin, choose the small town of Yangshuo. It's much more secluded and is famous for its breathtaking natural beauty, nestled as it is alongside the Li River and surrounded by mountains. Yet it has all the creature comforts of nice hotels and picturesque cafes with Western-style treats.

2. Huangshan (Huang Mountains) in Anhui Province

The Huang Mountains are a mountain range in southern Anhui Province in eastern China. The area is well known for its scenery, including numerous peculiarly shaped granite peaks and picturesque pine trees. The mountains are a frequent subject of traditional Chinese paintings and literature. This nature reserve can only be reached by cablecar or by climbing up the slopes. No vehicles are allowed, so this is one place in China where you can escape the congestion, pollution, and noise of traffic and stand and gaze in wonder at nature's beauty and majesty.

3. Wulingyuan National Park in Zhangjiajie, Hunan Province

This national park is a scenic and historical interest area in the small city of Zhangjiajie in Hunan Province. It's justly famous for its three thousand quartzite sandstone pillars, some of which are over eight hundred meters in height. These strange-shaped but majestic rock formations in a lush sub-tropical setting were the inspiration for the landscapes in the movie *Avatar*. Unfortunately, few Western tourists ever visit Wulingyuan.

4. Jiuzhaigou National Park in Sichuan Province

Jiuzhaigou Valley is a nature reserve located in China's Sichuan

Province. A beautiful example of China's varied landscape, Jiuzhaigou is famous for crystal-blue lakes and multi-tiered waterfalls. Here you'll also find a number of Tibetan villages, where you can see and experience Tibetan local culture.

5. The Three Gorges on the Yangtze River

Take a tour boat down the Yangtze River to enjoy the Three Gorges, which together are nearly 120 miles long. The majestic scenery along the river has been a source of inspiration for poets and artists in China over the centuries. The Three Gorges area offers a great variety of ecological environments and wildlife. Three Gorges Dam is a marvel of contemporary engineering, however controversial; it is the world's largest as well as the world's biggest hydroelectric power station. The river itself is the world's third longest, but the Three Gorges is by far the most spectacular part of any Yangtze River cruise.

6. West Lake in Hangzhou, Zhejiang Province

Scenic West Lake in the lovely city of Hangzhou is surrounded by mountains on three sides, with an area of around two square miles. Along the nine miles of its periphery you'll find beautiful gardens and pagodas. West Lake is also associated with many famous historical figures. The ancient buildings, stone caves, and engraved tablets in surrounding areas are among the most cherished national treasures of China.

7. Lushan National Park in Jiangxi Province

Lushan National Park in Jiangxi Province covers 320 square miles and has more than ninety mountain peaks that rise to heights of nearly 5,000 feet. Mt. Lu is famous for its steep slopes and spectacular scenery that includes ravines, waterfalls, and grottoes. There are a dozen main scenic areas to enjoy.

8. Mt. Emei in Sichuan Province

At 10,000 feet high, Mt. Emei in Sichuan Province is the tallest and arguably most beautiful of the Four Sacred Buddhist Mountains of China. It is also notable for its exceptionally diverse vegetation, ranging from sub-tropical to sub-alpine pine forests. Some of the trees here are more than a thousand years old. There are many cultural treasures nearby, most remarkably the Giant Buddha at Leshan. Carved out of the cliff face and standing well over 200 feet high, it guards the three rivers that join below its feet and is the tallest Buddha in the world.

9. Tiger Leaping Gorge and the Ancient Village of Lijiang in Yunnan Province

Tiger Leaping Gorge in Yunnan Province is one of the deepest river canyons in the world. It was carved by a river that flows in a series of rapids between two of China's tallest mountains. The steep cliffs on either side now rise 6,000 feet above the river. The name Tiger Leaping Gorge derives from the legend of a tiger that supposedly leapt over the river to escape a hunter.

The Naxi minority people who inhabit this area occupy a small group of villages. If you're really adventurous and physically fit, consider hiking along the gorge. Follow the well-kept path that's used by the natives on a daily basis. It's well marked, although very narrow in spots.

For those less inclined to great physical exertion, nearby is the lovely and quaint ancient village of Lijiang. The city is nearly eight hundred years old but beautifully preserved. Streams coming from the Jade River form canals and waterways that flow along the old town streets. When you climb up to the park above the village, you can see majestic mountains in the distance, including the Jade Dragon Snow Mountain.

10. The Himalayas in Tibet

The Himalayas are aptly called the Roof of the World, as they form the highest plateau in the world; the average elevation is over 16,000 feet. The Chinese part of the Himalayas is in the Autonomous Region of Tibet. The Trans-Himalayan drive of over 600 miles takes you through four mountainous passes and offers a panoramic view of the scenery and of the Tibetan way of life. Go only between late April and early November!

Our Favorite Books
and Movies about China

The following books and films will all help give you some perspective on the complex and rapidly changing society that is China. Most of them will show you China as it is now. Some will show you how China was in the recent past, so that you will know how fast and how far the country has come in one generation. The books are all well-written and engrossing reads, and in paperback form extremely affordable. In the likely event that you won't be able to read them all before you go, at least read one or two prior to your China adventure, and then enjoy the others after you've experienced the country for yourself. The movies from China as well as the documentary films about China produced in the West will give you other insights into this complex and fascinating country, including a visual picture of life there. Most of these movies and films are available from your local public library, and can also be purchased from the Internet for very reasonable prices.

Books about Contemporary China

1. *China Road: A Journey into the Future of a Rising Power* by Rob Gifford (2007)

National Public Radio China correspondent Gifford traveled for six weeks on a road that's a major artery of China, from its beginning in Shanghai for nearly three thousand miles to a tiny town in what was formerly called Turkestan. Having lived in China for many years and fluent in Chinese, Gifford talked to people from all walks of life along the way, including truck drivers, peasants, and even a hermit, to get a feel for what life is like in today's China. Great insights into how China's history shaped the way it is today, as well as summing up the country's greatest problems. If you only read one book about China today, make it this one.

2. *China Shakes the World: A Titan's Rise and Troubled Future— and the Challenge for America* by James Kynge (2007)

This book, by the *Financial Times*'s former Beijing bureau chief, gives a balanced and detailed picture of China's strengths and weaknesses in its recent emergence as a major economic and political force in the world. The book is full of interesting facts, figures, and stories about China's recent rapid economic growth.

3. *The Great Wall: China Against the World, 1000 BC — AD 2000* by Julia Lovell (2007)

Read a fascinating history of the Great Wall throughout the past three thousand years, and what the Wall has meant and still means to China. A Chinese history professor at Cambridge,

Lovell uses the Great Wall to give an insightful overview of Chinese history as well as of the Chinese psyche.

4. *River Town: Two Years on the Yangtze* by Peter Hessler (2001; reprinted in 2006)

A young American who spent two years teaching English in a small town on the Yangtze, Hessler comments on the major events in China at the end of the twentieth century, while showing us how those larger political events affected the lives of ordinary people. This book allows us to see a town in the hinterland of China whose people represent the majority of the population left behind in China's "economic miracle." This was the first of three insightful and popular books Hessler has written about the China that tourists rarely see.

5. *Country Driving: A Journey Through China from Farm to Factory* by Peter Hessler (2010)

Hessler in recent years has become a reporter for the *New Yorker*, and has been living and observing China for fifteen years now. Making a similar journey to Rob Gifford's in *China Road*, Hessler took to the roads in China, traveling on dirt tracks to the desert edges of the country as well as on brand-new highways to the new factory towns created during China's recent economic boom. In this, his latest book on China, he gives a balanced picture of how far and how fast China has modernized in certain cities while the rest of the country seems mired in a previous century.

6. *Serve the People: A Stir-Fried Journey Through China* by Jen Lin-liu (2008)

A Chinese-American, journalist, food writer, and now cooking school owner, Jen knew little about cooking when she came to China in 2000. She soon realized that food was such an integral part of Chinese life, she would better understand the culture if she understood the food. In a humorous way, Jen tells of her experiences in a Beijing vocational cooking school, at a noodle stall, and finally in Shanghai at a fancy restaurant. In the process she shares the insights she gained about everyday life in China's cities, not to mention the overview of the endlessly varied and fascinating cuisine of China.

7. *Coming Home Crazy: An Alphabet of China Essays* by Bill Holm (1990; reprinted in 2000)

Holm, a professor of literature at a college in Minnesota, went to China in the 1980s, near the beginning of China's dramatic "Reform and Opening Up," when China was just beginning to emerge from being one of the poorer and more repressive societies in the world and open itself up to the world. The other books on our reading list will give you a picture of contemporary China, but Bill Holm's book will show you how far and how fast China has come in less than one generation. And it's the most entertaining as well as most poetically written of all books on China. Best of all, it's written by a man with a big heart for the Chinese people and a great joie de vivre.

Arranged by the letters of the alphabet, with at least one entry per letter, these short pieces capture the variety of daily life in the China of the 1980s. Writing about traditions that endured in rural areas as well as many bureaucratic absurdities, Holm covers such topics as dumpling making, bound feet, Chinglish, night soil, banking, and the shoddiness of almost everything in daily life, from bicycles to elevators, which required constant repairs. This is a delightful book by a marvelous writer and a great human being.

Books about Chinese Society, Past and Present

1. *Wild Swans: Three Daughters of China* by Jung Chang (1991)
In a gripping way, Jung Chang tells the story of how three generations of women in her family fared in the political maelstrom of China during the twentieth century. Their lives reflect the most dramatic changes in the social position of women greater, perhaps, than those in any other society in history. Chang's grandmother was a warlord's concubine. Her mother, raised in a privileged household, rose to a prominent position in the Communist Party before being denounced during the Cultural Revolution. After leaving China in disillusionment over Mao's destructive policies, Jung Chang became a successful Chinese-American writer. This book provides a look at the personal, intimate side of Chinese family life throughout the twentieth century.

2. *Spring Moon: A Novel of China* by Bette Bao Lord (1981; reprinted in 2004)

Much like *Wild Swans*, this book uses the story of a woman named Spring Moon to deliver up a fascinating look at the history of China from the 1890s through the mid-1900s in a personal narrative from an endearing character. We experience events through the eyes of Spring Moon herself, who begins the novel as a young girl and who grows up to experience the many upheavals of revolution and war during the first half of the twentieth century in China.

3. *A Daughter of Han: The Autobiography of a Chinese Working Woman* by Ida Pruitt (1945)

This book is the memoir of a poor Chinese woman called only "Old Mrs. Ning." It was transcribed by an American, Ida Pruitt, over a two-year period from 1936–38, from her conversations with Mrs. Ning, who tells of her difficult life, taking us through her childhood, marriage, and various jobs working for both Chinese government officials and foreign missionaries. There is an extraordinary amount of detail about the life of a poor, working woman in the waning days of the last imperial dynasty. This is a special opportunity to see what life was like for the working classes in China before the Communist revolution, and to learn the sad plight of most women in traditional society.

Books about the Cultural Revolution (China's Holocaust)

It is impossible for Westerners to fully understand how much freer and more prosperous China is today than just one generation ago if they know nothing of the tumultuous and oppressive period of the Cultural Revolution that gripped the country from 1966–1976. Here are the best books on the subject, of which most of us in the West know far too little.

1. *China: Alive in the Bitter Sea* by Fox Butterfield (1982)

Butterfield helps us understand the magnitude of suffering that an estimated two hundred million people endured during this tumultuous and tragic period of Chinese history that only ended in the mid-'70s. The book touches us through the stories of the Chinese with whom Butterfield spoke shortly after the Cultural Revolution ended and whose personal experiences reflect the suffering of countless other Chinese.

2. *Son of the Revolution* by Liang Heng and Judith Shapiro (1984)

This book is the autobiographical experiences of Liang Heng, who grew up in the turmoil of the Great Cultural Revolution. Although his story is unique, it is in many ways typical of those millions of young Chinese whose lives were turned upside down during this period of chaos and madness. Through his words we hear an entire generation speaking, and come to understand why in China they are known as "The Lost Generation."

Documentary Films about China Today

1. *China Rises: A Documentary in Four Parts* (2008), 264 minutes

This compelling four-part series provides us with examples of China's rapid evolution from a secluded, backward country to an economic power much involved with the rest of the world. The film takes us across the country, from the Gobi Desert to a factory floor, from the Shanghai Film Festival to a pop concert at the Great Wall, from police rescuing abducted women to the training of astronauts. The film highlights the rapid pace of change in China today.

2. *China Today: Issues that Trouble Americans at the Start of the 21st Century* (2008), 63 minutes

During the summers of 2005 and 2006, the authors of *China Survival Guide* traveled around China to discover the consequences of the economic and political reforms in the past few decades in the lives of the Chinese people. We also wanted to find answers to the basic questions that have troubled our students about China, such as "Will China become a democracy any time soon?" "How severe and cruel is the so-called 'one-child policy'?" "How much religious freedom is there really in China when there are so many 'underground churches' and we hear about the persecution of church leaders?"

The film can be viewed for free on the Calvin College website, www.calvin.edu, A-Z Index, Calvin Media Foundation, or can be purchased for $10 from the Calvin College Bookstore www.calvin.edu, A-Z Index, Bookstore.

We conducted interviews with Chinese people from different walks of life, including college professors and other educators, free-thinking writers and intellectuals, marriage and family experts, and religious leaders, but also peasants and migrant workers and shop clerks. The film also features extensive video footage of daily life in China in the middle of the first decade of the twenty-first century.

Our hope is that this film will help correct some of the distorted impressions Americans have about contemporary China and lead to a greater understanding of life in the world's most populous country.

We are currently producing a second documentary film entitled *What the Chinese Think of Us (and What We Think of Them)*, which should be available by the fall of 2011. This second film is based on interviews we conducted in 2009 and 2010 in China with Chinese people from various walks of life as to how they viewed the U.S. and Americans. We also interviewed Americans from Oregon to Georgia as to how they viewed China and the Chinese. Our attempt is to expose the potential dangers of the considerable misunderstandings on both sides, especially on the part of many Americans.

3. *Heart of the Dragon* (1984), 12 hours

This series was filmed by a BBC film crew over several years and presents a rare portrait of how life was lived in China in the early 1980s, just when China was opening up to the rest of the world. Each of the twelve episodes focuses on a universal aspect of life and profiles the Chinese people themselves, from peasants to factory workers, from Communist Party leaders to artists, scientists, and millionaires. The first six episodes include: (1) Remembering—An overview of historic and modern China, exploring famine, invasion, civil war, and the Cultural Revolution. (2) Caring—Focuses on the family. (3) Eating—Methods of food production to support a population that continues to grow at an alarming rate. (4) Believing—Influence of traditional and modern doctrines—Taoism, Buddhism, Confucianism, Marxism, and Maoism. (5) Correcting—Chinese legal system. (6) Working—Lives of China's industrial workers. Later episodes deal with Marriage, the Arts, etc.

It is unfortunate that there exists no such comprehensive documentary of life in contemporary China. However, this series is beautifully and sensitively done, with commentary at the end of each episode from famous people ranging from Bette

Bao Lord to Henry Kissinger. Its value lies in showing the startling contrast between China today and the China that existed only three decades ago. This film documents the fact that truly no society in the history of the world has ever undergone such a dramatic transformation in so short a time as has China in the past generation.

This BBC series is available only in VHS from your public library or from www.amazon.com in individual episodes.

Chinese Feature Films
1. *To Live* directed by Zhang Yimou (1998; released on DVD in 2003)

Zhang Yimou is arguably the greatest filmmaker in China and one of the world's great cinematographers. It was Zhang who choreographed the stunning opening ceremony for the Beijing Olympics in 2008. Perhaps more famous for his blockbuster films, *Hero* and *House of Flying Daggers*, his "art films" are among the best products of Chinese cinema.

It's difficult to choose just one of Zhang Yimou's profound and moving films, but should you only see one Chinese feature film, choose *To Live*. Personal and political events are interwoven, as we follow the struggles of an impoverished husband and wife from their pampered life in the 1930s to the hardships that they experience during the Cultural Revolution in the 1960s. They raise two children during this tumultuous period, surviving numerous setbacks and yet managing, somehow, to continue to live. Both intimate and epic, Zhang's film encompasses the simplest and most profound realities of Chinese life during this tragic period. The movie stars the beautiful and emotive Gong Li, who plays the heroine in the vast majority of Zhang Yimou's films.

2. *The Road Home* directed by Zhang Yimou (1999; released on DVD in 2001)

A young man returns to his native village after the death of his father, the village schoolteacher. His body lies in a neighboring town, where his father had gone to raise money for a new schoolhouse. The mother of the young man insists that her husband be brought back to his home village for burial on foot, lest his spirit be unable to find the way home. Most of the movie is about the young man's recounting of his parents' courtship, which resulted in the first marriage in their village based on love rather than an arrangement by the respective families. You'll perhaps recognize the actress, Zhang Ziyi, who plays the mother as a young woman, from her starring role in the movie *Crouching Tiger, Hidden Dragon*.

3. *Shower* (2000)

This is a simply told but heartwarming story about an aging

father and his men-
tally handicapped son
who run one of the
last public bathhouses
in Beijing. When the
estranged older son,
a successful business-
man in Shanghai, is
lured into returning home for a visit, he
gradually comes to see how much the bathhouse means to the
local community. While affirming the bonds of family and of
friends, the film also shows another example of the sea changes
in Chinese society in recent times. The fast pace of modernization, with high-rise apartments replacing the old one-story
alleyway dwellings in Beijing, has meant the disappearance of
tight-knit communities and spelled the death for the traditional bathhouses where the men of the community would gather.
The destruction of the old neighborhoods has been so rapid
that the filmmaker could not find one public bathhouse left in
Beijing and had to film this movie in a different city!

4. *Postmen in the Mountains* (1998; released as a DVD in 2004)
This little-known film is in the same gentle and loving vein as
Shower, and also centers around family relationships. The movie
is the story of an aging postman, who for over two decades has
been trekking through the mountains on a sixty-kilometer route
in order to deliver mail to the people in the remote rural areas of

Hunan Province. He has always done the route alone, accompanied only by his faithful dog, a lovely German shepherd. His son, now in his early twenties, has always resented the fact that his father was generally absent from home while he was growing up. The father, however, hopes that his recalcitrant son will take over his job, now that the aging man's knees are giving out and he'll soon be unable to make his arduous rounds.

His son reluctantly agrees to join his father on the last trip his Dad will ever make. On the way, like the older son in the movie *Shower*, this son comes to realize how much his father's work has meant in the lives of the villagers to whom he has delivered the mail for so long. This film is just as heartwarming a film as *Shower*, and includes stunning scenery in the mountainous areas of the Hunan countryside.

Topic Index

ABOUT THE AUTHORS

Larry Herzberg is a professor at Calvin College
in Grand Rapids, Michigan. Since 1984, he has
taught first- through fourth-year Chinese language courses, as well as several courses on
Chinese culture and society. In 2011, he was
awarded the Presidential Award for Exem-
plary Teaching, the highest honor that Calvin
College bestows on a faculty member. Larry has visited mainland China numerous times over the past twenty-five years. He is also a full-time violinist
with the Grand Rapids Symphony.

Qin Xue Herzberg grew up in Beijing and is a graduate of Beijing Normal University, where she majored in Chinese literature. For the past ten years she has
taught upper-level Chinese language courses at Calvin College. She has written articles for several of China's most popular magazines, including *Marriage
and the Family and China Educator's Journal*. She has also published articles in
America's leading Chinese newspaper, *World Journal*.

Larry and Qin have produced two documentary films on contemporary China.
The first, released in 2008, is entitled *China Today: Issues That Trouble Americans at the Start of the 21st Century*. In 2012 they released a 2½-hour film called
The China Threat: Perception versus Reality. Several thousand copies of both films
have been distributed to colleges, universities and high schools all across the
United States and Canada, as well as to public libraries, thanks to funding from
the David and Shirley Hubers Asian Studies Program of Calvin College. These
films are available through the Calvin Media Foundation of Calvin College.

The couple received grants from the National Endowment for the Humanities
as well as the Hubers Asian Studies Program to return to China in the summers
of 2012 and 2013 to film a documentary about the major dialects of Chinese and
their effect on the varied pronunciation of the national language of Mandarin
across China.